ANNA WILLIAMSON
WITH DR. REETTA NEWELL

BREAKING
MUM AND
DAD

THE INSIDER'S GUIDE TO PARENTING ANXIETY

GREEN TREE

LONDON · OXFORD · NEW YORK · NEW DELHI · SYDNEY

GREEN TREE
Bloomsbury Publishing Plc
50 Bedford Square, London, WC1B 3DP, UK

BLOOMSBURY, GREEN TREE and the Green Tree logo are trademarks of
Bloomsbury Publishing Plc

First published in Great Britain 2018

A catalogue record for this book is available from the British Library

Library of Congress Cataloguing-in-Publication data has been applied for

ISBN: PB: 978-1-4729-5335-3; eBook: 978-1-4729-5336-0

2 4 6 8 10 9 7 5 3 1

Designed by Verlag by Deanta Global Publishing Services, Chennai, India
Printed and bound in Great Britain by CPI Group (UK) Ltd. Croydon, CRO 4YY

To find out more about our authors and books visit www.bloomsbury.com
and sign up for our newsletters

CONTENTS

PREFACE

Before I became a mum I used to scoff at people who cited parenthood as 'the hardest job in the world'... pah! What, sitting at home watching daytime telly in your PJs, cuddling a scrummy sleeping baby? Do me a favour – it sounded like bliss, a doss, a total result. Fast forward several years, and oh how I came down off my high horse!

27 September 2016 is a very special day for me. It's the day I officially lost my independent, 'it's just me' status, and became a mother. A day I had been waiting for – for more than 20 years. I always knew I wanted, *needed*, to be a mum. As a kids' television presenter and counsellor people often remarked that I'd 'be a natural', and I totally believed them.

However, as I discovered, entertaining other people's children on TV is an entirely different kettle of fish to making, birthing and rearing your own child. It's safe to say that my launch into motherhood was not easy. In fact, I'd go as far as to say it was pretty bloody traumatic. The birth was hands down the hardest thing I have ever encountered, but hey, it's called labour for a reason I guess. But it was the days, weeks and months after my son arrived that really challenged me beyond anything I could have imagined – not just physically, but emotionally and mentally.

In those long, sleep-deprived early weeks, I felt anxiety, terror, loneliness and low mood like I've never known – and that's saying something. I've had a well-documented history of mental health blips – my first book, *Breaking Mad: The Insider's Guide To Conquering Anxiety*, can fill you in on all that.

Thankfully, I knew what to do and where to go to get immediate support and help for the debilitating feelings I was experiencing. I am one of the lucky ones. But there are millions of new mums, and dads, who also feel like the rug has been well and truly pulled out from under their feet the moment they become a parent. Indeed, during the research for this book I delved into other parents' innermost thoughts, feelings and behaviours and discovered just how many of us are suffering in silence, afraid of being judged for not being 'supermum' or 'perfect dad', and not loving *every* minute.

Breaking Mum and Dad: The Insider's Guide to Parenting Anxiety is for every parent, grandparent, adoptive parent, step-parent, foster parent... (you get my drift) out there. Parenting is hard enough without keeping the festering feelings and thoughts inside, to fester away some more. This book is for us all. It includes bits of my personal story of my foray into motherhood, along with the stories of other parents along the way. Mums of multiples, single dads, surrogate parents, same-sex parents, adoptive mothers, stepmums, IVF couples... I embarked on a quest to get answers from lots of parents and lots of different demographics, not just the traditional 'mum and dad' set-up.

It doesn't matter *how* you get your precious baby, we are all one and the same – we are parents going through the same emotions, the good *and* the bad.

This sanity-saving guide reveals how it can *really* feel to be a new mum and dad, and celebrates the highs and the lows. I'll explore some of the conditions that can occur after birth, such as post-natal depression and anxiety, and birth trauma, and take a peek into the pressures of making new mum friends, dealing with next to no sleep, coping with unwanted advice, the 'going back to work' anxiety, and of course the infamous 'mum guilt'.

We've probably all got the books on 'how to change a nappy', 'sleep training ideas' and 'when to wean' – books I couldn't have done without – but *this* book is about the *other* non-physical stuff. The stuff that can make us feel stir crazy, a bag of hormones, and unsure of which way to turn. Along with my parent pals and my wonderful friend Dr Reetta Newell – who as well as being a top-notch Clinical Psychologist is also a mum of two young girls – my aim is for you to feel supported, understood and, above all, like you're not alone. Because, trust me, whatever you're feeling, good or bad, there are a gazillion others experiencing exactly the same thing.

Being a parent is one of the most life-changing, challenging yet rewarding and wonderful things we can do. There is nothing quite like it.

So, welcome to your support group, your 'go to' for when the feelings and emotions get a bit weird and need explaining, for those moments of 'Help! I want a day off from this parenting job!' You will find no cliquey judging here, you will hear from parents like you who are going through the motions too... and you never know, we might just make you smile a bit as we go.

Dr Reetta and I will also share some helpful and *easy* (we know how hard it can be to concentrate when you've got a screaming banshee time bomb about to go off in the next room) exercises and activities to help you relax, understand yourself better, and provide a bit of timely motivation and empowerment.

Throughout the book you will find 'Breaking Point SOS' handy hints, 'How to...' ideas, and 'Activity Alerts' to help you get through the tough days. What's more, at the end of each chapter you'll get some valuable advice from 'Dr Reetta Says'. We hope you find our research, anecdotes and advice empathetic, sympathetic and ultimately helpful.

INTRODUCTION
OH S**T, WHAT HAVE WE DONE?

'Don't worry Ms Williamson, just because this birth didn't quite go the way you wanted it to, it doesn't mean you can't try again one day.' Not exactly the magical first words I'd dreamed of hearing after the birth of my son. And as for the labour not going 'quite' the way I'd hoped... well if that wasn't the understatement of the century I don't know what was!

So how did I get here? Before we get into the practical stuff, I wanted to share my pregnancy and birth story with you – so that you know where I'm coming from, and because I asked so many other people to be brave and share their stories with me, too. I hope it helps – remember, we're all in this together!

I'd entered the no-man's-land of pregnancy with trepidation, excitement and no idea about what the next nine months would hold, with the actual physical task of getting the baby out being just too mind-blowing to comprehend. So, I did what every mature and sensible woman does: I initially buried my head in the sand. I wouldn't say I'm a naïve person, but I somehow foolishly convinced myself that being pregnant would be like the movies, with a weightless 'beach ball' bump shoved neatly up my jumper, showcasing my newly voluptuous figure, with the actual 'getting sprog out' being merely a polite cough, a teeny 'straining for a poo' groan, and then... ta-daa... hello baby. Cue the obligatory schmaltzy Facebook post and off we go.

Oh how wrong I was. The harsh reality was that I really didn't enjoy pregnancy. I can't say I *hated* it, there were definite moments of happiness/anticipation, but on the whole, I felt sick, heavy, hot (not in the sexy sense), and the actual labour and birth experience was definitely one of my top-five most un-fun things to do ever. From the moment I saw the positive result on the pregnancy test my ecstatic joy was instantly masked with a niggle of worry... As someone who'd suffered for years with anxiety and panic disorder I always knew that I was a candidate for prenatal and post-natal depression and anxiety, so from the beginning I was aware that I needed to take good care of my mental, as well as physical, health. The overwhelming responsibility I felt for both of us was, well, *completely* overwhelming!

Armed with my 'golden ticket' (the positive wee stick) I hotfooted it down to see my GP and get some much-needed advice on what the heck to do now I was pregnant, and still taking a low dosage of anti-anxiety medication. My plan had originally been to come off the medication before we started trying but clearly Santa Claus was destined to give us a joint present that year (yep we actually conceived on Christmas Eve) so I never actually had a chance to reduce and come off the meds gradually – which is usually recommended.

I was advised by my doctor to come off the pills as soon as possible in order to guard against growth and development problems in my three-week-old foetus. And there, in that little clinic, my anxiety was re-ignited... 'What if I've damaged the baby already?', 'What if my anxiety returns?' Hmm, never mind the new baby, a whole new breed of anxiety was born.

It didn't help that I had terrible morning sickness (how annoying is it when people say 'ooh that's a good sign'? At the time I just wanted to not feel so darn awful and be able to eat anything other than Birds Eye Fish Fingers and baked beans). A few months into my pregnancy, and with no medication crutch, I began to feel those familiar feelings of dread, worry and unexplained loneliness creep in. I was also extremely irritable and irrational at times, but people often just brush this aside and blame hormones.

The NHS antenatal team put me on a special list, and gave me an appointment with an Obstetrics and Gynaecology (Ob/Gyn) Consultant who was tasked with keeping an eye on my mental health. At my first appointment I was asked questions about how I was feeling about my unborn baby and impending motherhood. I obviously passed the test and seemed pretty together because I was deemed fit and well and released back to the standard midwifery team. Hurrah.

But looking back, I'm not sure whether or not I felt a stigma attached to being pregnant and fears of being judged an unfit mother due to my mental health history. In all honesty, I think I felt that I had to be fit and healthy in all ways or else people would think that I couldn't do this. The NHS care team really were lovely and very supportive (massive shout out to my angel of a community midwife Julie), but I put way too much pressure on myself to suddenly be this 'Mary Poppins' expectant mother – ie unrealistically perfect in every way! Everyone just assumes you must be loving every second of carrying your child, and the truth was that I felt so rough I just wasn't enjoying it, and was too scared to admit this to anyone out of sheer guilt. After all, how many people struggle to get pregnant and here I was with an easily conceived honeymoon baby growing in my tummy. And there it is, that word GUILT – a word all parents are so familiar with – and I felt it way before my son was even a fully formed foetus. So really, what chance did I have, eh?

With the months ticking past, agonisingly slowly, the impending unknown of giving birth felt even more terrifying. 'How will it get out?', 'What if it doesn't fit?', 'How bad will the pain be?'... as time went on I read every book going, scoured NetMums and BabyCentre forums daily, took hypnobirthing and NCT classes to prepare me for the task ahead... by 40 weeks I felt I knew it all... yet nothing, NOTHING, could have prepared me for what was to come.

Forty hours of labour. Back to back contractions, more drugs than you could shake a stick at, two epidurals, a spinal block, episiotomy, and a forceps delivery... in a haze of semi-consciousness I delivered a healthy baby boy. Ta-daaaaaaa... and my initial feelings: nothing other than sheer shock.

Where there 'should' have been a flood of love and overwhelming joy, there was nothing. It was like my emotional plug socket had been yanked out of the wall and stamped on. The disappointment at my zero feelings was just terrifying. I could hear the baby crying from somewhere in the room and I remember feeling an instinct to protect him (at least I felt *something*), but as I lay there exhausted all I really felt was an overwhelming feeling of sadness, detachment and disappointment – not in my son I hasten to add, but by the way he came into the world. Nine months of my husband and I fantasising about meeting our little baby (we deliberately hadn't found out the gender as we wanted the surprise of discovering it together in a *Lion King*-style presentation) and celebrating with the first joint cuddle, was, in my eyes, ruined.

As I lay there with doctors sorting out the battle zone that was my privates, the shock at what had just happened was almost too much to bear. And now, as if that wasn't bad enough, I had to look after a little baby from scratch. Cue my anxiety relapse, BIG TIME!!

This is the start of my journey: after birth. I find so much is focused in the news and media on the *practicalities* of new parenting – and don't get me wrong, this is seriously important; without several books, apps and websites I'd have been clueless about how to bathe my newborn, or how to ease his colic – but nothing prepared me for just how crap it can feel emotionally and mentally, and how in the space of a day I could go from a confident, independent career woman to a hapless, terrified, emotional wreck that I didn't even recognise as being myself.

This, my friends, my wonderfully brilliant fellow new parents, is the book in which we all make sense of those weird, wonderful, terrifying and traumatic feelings, thoughts and behaviours that can affect us all at some point along the way from those first newborn days to the months ahead of learning how to juggle and embrace this fabulous, scary new role.

You are among friends. It's time to realise that you are not only doing a great job as a parent, but that you are also totally normal to not love it ALL the time.

Grab a cuppa and a (packet of) biscuits, and let's share this experience together...

Anna x

1
THE DAY AFTER BIRTH

The 'what just happened?' feeling

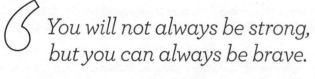

You will not always be strong, but you can always be brave.

Beau Taplin

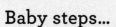
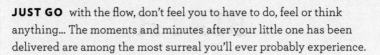

Baby steps...

JUST GO with the flow, don't feel you to have to do, feel or think anything... The moments and minutes after your little one has been delivered are among the most surreal you'll ever probably experience.

TAKE WHATEVER time you need to recover from your birthing experience. Everyone is different so listen to your mind, emotions and body and go at *your* pace.

DRINK (LOTS!) of tea/chai latte/hot chocolate and eat as much toast as you like – you've earned it! The tastiest and most deserved thing that'll ever pass your lips... and it really does help... even just a little bit.

Woah, what the hell just happened?

'Well, bugger me with a fish fork!' Forgive me for stealing one of my favourite *Blackadder* quotes, but no other words could do this situation justice. If I hadn't laughed, I would certainly have cried. And I may never have stopped.

I had just accomplished the one thing I had fantasised about for decades. Nine months of sicky burps, uncontrollable flatulence and a bump the size of a double-decker bus had finally ended. I had actually done it – I had given birth to a healthy baby boy! And here starts my journey into what happens next.

Now, before I go any further, I just need to clear a few things up. Throughout this book, I'm going to make a few assumptions. I hope that's OK. I am assuming you're reading this book because you're curious about the 'other' side of giving birth, and what becoming a freshly turned-out parent can be *really* like. We're going to talk about the physical stuff too (after all, childbirth is undoubtedly a challenge physically) but what we're really going to be delving into is the mental health and emotional well-being side of parenting. I'm guessing that if you're already on the other side then becoming a mum or dad has been a big shock to your system, too, and at times you really don't know your arse from your elbow. I'm also assuming that you've been experiencing certain thoughts, feelings and behaviours, no matter how small or fleeting, that have worried you and/or made you feel like the biggest loner and phoney in the world. Perhaps you've felt like a caged tiger, trapped and craving to get the hell outta there – 'there' meaning parent-ville – even just for five minutes so that you can take a deep breath and get yourself together. Maybe you've questioned your ability to care for and rear another human being – *your* human being? Well, my friend, if any of this has provoked even the most tentative spark of recognition then you are in good company – because I pretty much felt, and still feel at times, all of the above. And we're not alone either.

I want to reassure you now, before we go any further, that it's totally *OK*, and you are completely and utterly *normal*. In fact, The National Childbirth Trust (NCT) recently reported that around half of all new mothers' post-natal mental health problems don't get picked up on, and with more than 50 per cent of all new mothers experiencing a mental or emotional issue either during pregnancy and/or post birth – the stats speak volumes. So, trust me, we're all in the same boat, navigating the same unchartered waters (and occasionally feeling like we are drowning).

There are, of course, some parents who have textbook births, perfect children and just love every minute (even embracing the dreaded sleep deprivation as 'more precious time to spend with my little one'). I'm all for praising the sisterhood and I genuinely love that some people can breeze into becoming parents and are spared the other, slightly (er very!) rubbish feelings that the weeks after birth can bring. It gives me hope that it can be OK.

But I'm guessing those lucky devils aren't going to be grasping this book with a shaky hand, (possible) medicinal glass of vino in the other, squinting at it through eye bags the size of steamer trunks. The rest of us are looking for some empathy and reassurance that we're not failing at our new job, and are not actually going mad.

Parenting is unlike any other life experience, career choice or vocation you could ever conjure up in your wildest dreams. The books and classes try to prepare you, and some do a pretty good job, but it's just not the same as the wallop of 'baby day' when it actually happens. It is wonderful and rewarding in so many ways, but it is also shit scary a lot of the time.

'When my daughter finally arrived I think I was just majorly relieved. I'd had a terrible birth and it was the complete opposite to what I'd planned and hoped for. I wanted a water birth on the midwife-led unit and to go home as soon as possible. I actually ended up being induced and almost three days later she arrived via emergency C-section and had to stay in hospital for three full days after!! Either way she was just perfect.'

Bronwen – mum to Georgia, aged 10 months

The curse of the birth plan

One of the most weird (and utterly terrifying) things to contemplate for me, once I was in the family way, was how on earth I was going to give birth to a whole new person. It was pretty easy getting it 'in' (sorry, TMI), but a very different ball game getting it out...

Now, you may be reading this having just had a baby – the memory still fresh as a daisy – or perhaps you're not quite at this stage yet and still in the throes of making babies/pregnancy with all this to come, in which case hopefully this bit will save you a lot of unnecessary angst. Or maybe your birth is a distant memory – if so, I'm certain this will raise a knowing smile, or wince, of recognition.

It seems that the minute you get pregnant all anyone in the know asks you (as well as the endless 'do you know what you're having?' question) is, 'ooh what's your birth plan?' What *is* our obsession with knowing how someone is going to birth their baby? Why do we care so much? I am completely guilty of asking pregnant friends (sometimes not even actual friends... people in the gym, supermarket etc) the same, extremely personal thing. I can't help myself. Are you having a water birth? Do you want pain relief? Who's going to cut the cord? We fire these deeply intimate questions out with genuine excitement and interest.

I like to think that ultimately it's not just because we are nosy sods, it's because we care about the expectant mother's experience. We *want* her to have a good one, we want the baby to arrive safely, and we want all to be well. And, oh alright then, we're just a teeny bit nosy and it says a smidgeon (a lot) about us too. The reason being, there's a niggling, fizzing, desperate-to-be-heard part of us that wants to share our own birth plans and experiences. We want to wear them like a badge of honour saying 'I did it too!' and 'we're in the same club!'

If you're anything like me, we're so interested in other people's experiences because we want to *compare*. We want to check that others might have opted for the same thing we did, and we just can't help throwing our opinion out – whether it's been asked for or not. We *want* to be asked how our births went and what choices we made, and now we have the birthing T-shirt we want to offer words of wisdom (subtle warning) to others about to go through the same experience based on our own experiential research. There's also a definite know-all attitude of 'I've been there' that we just cannot help but crow about (because giving birth is a massive deal). Asking the 'what's your birth plan' question is essentially a way of opening up a conversation that's actually a camouflaged counselling session.

The story of my birth plan

TALKING ABOUT our preferences for birth is one of the only things we can have full control over – when of course the reality is it's an unscripted chapter we have virtually *no* control over at all. I remember being counselled by the wise teacher in my NCT class not to overdo the birth plan and to ideally keep it to a side of A4 paper. A SIDE of A4 paper?! Many people's plans consist of three or four lines, mostly stating a preference for the where rather than the how, but mine started out as an epistle at 20 weeks, with all kinds of instructions (orders!) for the midwifery team...

1 'Ask not tell me' for pain relief.

2 I want to birth in the pool to soothing music with candles.

3 Ensure the baby has at LEAST 10 minutes of 'delayed cord clamping'.

4 Husband to announce the gender...

And so it went on. And on. In a moment of complete bossiness and madness, I even emailed the birth plan to my immediate family to instruct them, too (which to be fair did quite rightly prompt a LOT of teasing and sniggering). The end result? Well, you can see it coming a mile off really – not only did it bring on a whole fresh batch of anxiety that I really could have done without, but after all my obsessing and fantasising, said birth plan didn't even make it out of the hospital bag. In fact the doctors and midwives were given just one instruction as I was wheeled in, mooing like a cow... 'GIVE ME DRUGS!!!'

A birth plan then, for me, was a total waste of time and emotional energy. In fact, as I was carefully warned by said NCT teacher I set myself up for a massive fall when my birth didn't go even remotely to plan. I'm not saying that birth plans are a bad idea – I still happen to think they are really important as it's vital to let your birth partner (if you have one) and the team birthing your baby know any preferences you *might* have. It's just helpful to remember not to get too hung up on your carefully crafted, colour-coded and laminated birth plan document (yep, laminated. Seriously – what was I thinking!), and to accept that sometimes, things can't always be rigidly controlled – certainly, as I've learned, when it comes to Mother Nature.

> '*I was one of those people who decided not to have a birth plan, as I'd been told it never goes to plan. I'm very glad of this, as vomiting, epidurals, a spinal block and forceps would definitely have not been in any plan.*'
>
> **Amy – mum of nine-month-old Albie**

According to The Birth Trauma Association, there are at least 200,000 women each year who are left feeling traumatised by childbirth, but I feel it's important to highlight that lots of other women really *do* manage to have the births they've spent nine months dreaming of. These women are certainly fortunate in that they haven't had to deal with disappointment and trauma during labour and with any carefully honed plans being thrown out of the window, and instead are able to see their version of a 'good' birth through from start to finish. But even if you had a 'good' birth you can still have just as many anxieties and worries about all the other stuff that surrounds birth and being a new parent. So don't feel guilty and think you have to keep quiet about your positive birth experience – I know from friends that women in this situation often do. In fact, share it, especially with people who are pregnant for the first time – your tale of empowerment and the wonder of giving birth to a new person is inspiring and gives hope and courage to people who are likely to be fearful and fazed by the more common horror stories.

'*Physically I was knackered but emotionally I was on a serious high. I never had a birth plan as such, I just hoped for the best and when I look back, I thoroughly enjoy talking about it and some moments I will never forget.*'

Beth – mum to Arthur, Mary and 'bump number three'

Talking of birth horror stories, it's always amazing that these are worn like some kind of warped badge of honour by a few mums who are a little bit sneery about anyone who dares admit their experience was OK, even *nice* – I'll admit I was Miss 'My Birth Was Worse Than Yours' when I'd just had Enzo. Shouldn't we all just be praising everyone, patting backs and doffing caps to *anybody* who has undertaken the mammoth task of having a baby? Few of us get away with a 'perfect birth', and even those that do, well, I say good on you!

The bottom line is that we ALL worry. Worry about being honest, worry about being *dis*honest, worry about being judged, worry about looking like a clueless frazzled mess... Not one mum or dad I have spoken to has been left unscathed by parenting anxiety – it can hit us all, any time any place. I say it's time we all shared a bit of the love. Essentially we have all done the one thing in life that is so common (having a baby), yet completely unique to each of us. It might be that you're feeling a whole cocktail of emotions right now, and the main thing is to not measure yourself against anyone else or their experiences. These are *your* feelings and emotions, they are valid and are fully respected, and I want you to know that whatever stage you're at with getting your head around it all, there is no rush and we are all here to help in this book by way of sharing. I am on a mission to help everyone feel comfortable enough to understand their personal experiences, embrace them, and essentially be proud of them – whatever they may be.

The good, the bad and the unexpected

BEFORE I BECAME a mum I genuinely used to think having a baby was akin to having bad period pain – just pop a couple of painkillers, push like you're straining for a poo for a while, give a little yelp and then – tadaaaa!! – you had a baby. For me this rather nonchalant assumption couldn't have been further from the truth. In fact, I wasn't just living in cloud cuckoo land, I owned the whole sodding planet! I think regardless of the way my little boy came into this world, it would have been a shock, even if it had gone 'perfectly', and I know the common denominator among parents, regardless of their birth story, is the feeling of 'what the hell was that?!'

WHILE SOME births do go to plan, others are more unexpected – we've all heard stories of waters going in supermarket aisles, people having a boy when they were told they were having a girl, women giving birth in a lay-by en route to the hospital... that kind of thing. Some are downright shite birthing experiences with all manner of things going awry, and some special TLC may be required to help women to recover from them.

IN THOSE first few days, weeks and months many of us will experience a range of emotions, hopefully some of which are good ones, but they can leave us feeling anxious, tearful, worried, on edge and not knowing which way to turn. You may have had a 'good' birth, you may have had one that was a little unexpected or you may have had a total shocker... Whatever your experience, it doesn't matter in terms of what comes next. After birth day we are all one and the same – surfing a wave of emotion, plonked straight in the middle of an ocean treading water without a compass or lifejacket – and the only way through is to be as honest, open and brave as you can possibly be. It's going to be tough – but you're not alone! There are millions in the same boat – and I'm a fully signed up shipmate!

Going public

Regardless of how, when (you might be early or overdue) and where (on the kitchen floor anyone?) you give birth though, it's pretty much a forgone conclusion that you'll click into 'public face' mode almost instantly to crow about your new addition, because, well, that's kind of the done thing.

Activity alert

Bye bye 'blah' birth

This exercise is designed to help you let any negative feelings and thoughts go. It's proven that getting any angst and pent-up stress out of your head and either out in the open or down on paper can be hugely helpful in making peace with a situation.

If your birthing experience didn't go quite to plan, if you in some way mourn the birth you 'wish' you'd had, then this is your opportunity to get all that anger, regret, sadness, disappointment, negative energy and fed-up feelings out once and for all.

Take a piece of paper (or you can use your computer, tablet or phone if you prefer to type) and write the following heading: 'How I feel about my birth experience?'

You might like to doodle a thought bubble and then write words around it, or you might choose to draw a spider-gram and have this sentence in the middle of the paper, labelling the 'legs' around it. Or you might choose to write a letter to yourself. It's up to you, YOU are in charge.

You now have free rein to write, draw, scribble whatever you want in answer to the heading above… Let whatever comes into your mind just flow out on to the paper or screen.

Using words, thoughts, sentences, drawings, quotes – whatever feels natural and captures your experience – just go for it. You might even like to use colours or drawings if that feels right for you.

Once you've got it all out and down in front of you, if you feel comfortable doing so, read back all you've written to yourself and as you do so imagine that these feelings are about someone else. Allow yourself to detach emotionally from them as if you were letting them go and making peace. In your mind, keep increasing the 'distance' between you and these negative feelings, imagining anything unpleasant just floating away behind you.

Take a deep breath and as you exhale say to yourself 'it's over, and I have the most unique and incredible prize to show for my courage and hard work'.

Enjoy any feelings of peace, calm and lightness as you allow the negativity to just leave your mind and body.

You may like to go one step further and, if you've used a piece of paper, you may find it cathartic to screw it up and throw it in the bin to symbolise how you've got rid of any negative experience. Alternatively (my personal favourite), ensuring you're in a safe place burn the piece of paper, and as you watch the flames take hold imagine all that negativity going up in smoke, too.

Well done. Pat yourself on the back (and have a cuppa and piece of cake to celebrate).

If you're still left with any unhelpful feelings towards your birth, you might like to consider exploring a birth reflection, a service offered on the NHS to help parents talk through any negative experiences from their birth. See chapter 9 for more details.

It's become a tradition, hasn't it? The obligatory Facebook post announcing the new arrival. Unless you're super posh no one bothers with birth announcements in the newspaper any more (although my mum would have been all over this if I'd let her!), and doing a text and ring round is a bit of a time-consuming faff, so it's fast become the easiest way to post a quick status update to let everyone know that baby is here.

Now, I say 'quick' status update, but come on, who are we kidding? How much time and effort *really* goes in to carefully crafting and fine-tuning that momentous post? In my case pretty much all day, with me faffing about with the best filter and angle to eliminate eye bags and greasy hair as best as possible, before I would let my husband loose my missive into the abyss of cyberspace. I now *totally* get why Kate Middleton (allegedly) had a hairdresser to help sort her out and make her presentable for the world's media literally hours after her babies arrived. If she was anything like me post labour, she'd have looked a total state (although I suspect the Duchess of Cambridge could *actually* be Superwoman because surely no one is capable of looking *that* good, and able to stand 'legs together' so soon after giving birth...).

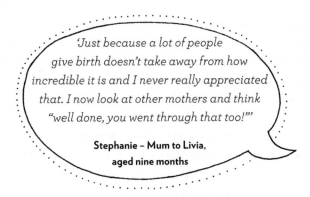

'Just because a lot of people give birth doesn't take away from how incredible it is and I never really appreciated that. I now look at other mothers and think "well done, you went through that too!"'

**Stephanie – Mum to Livia,
aged nine months**

There I was, 10 days overdue, after 40 hours of horrific labour that didn't go the way I'd even remotely imagined – no one 'dreams' of feeling like utter shite when they meet their baby for the first time – yet the minute I was wheeled into recovery, I chose to pose for my first picture with my baby boy. To say I didn't look my best really is an understatement – in fact I'm almost rather in awe of the blown-up-whale (fluid retention is a bitch!), red-faced, bird's-nest-hair, arms-full-of-wires sorry sight that greets me each time I reminisce over one particular photo that definitely did *not* get posted. 'Glowing' isn't the first word that comes to mind...

So, plastering on the best smile my weary face could muster, those first moments were captured on camera, and minutes later my waiting family and friends received a picture of mummy and baby to coo over. Ahhh lovely. Except it wasn't. And I'm not talking about the aesthetics now, I'm talking about how I was feeling.

How many times do we see posts from friends who have just joined the parents' club, with the obligatory: 'We are proud to announce the arrival of our new baby... born today at X o'clock. Mum and baby are doing well, we are so happy and totally overwhelmed with love for our new baby.'

Seriously, most of us are telling big fat porkies. I was that fibber, too. What a lot of new parents *actually* mean is: 'Thank f**k that ordeal is over with. I'm alive (just), my privates resemble a beaten-up lilo and my insides feel like a boxing bag, and all I want to do is sleep – alone – and for everyone to sod off.'

In my first sentence, the 'totally overwhelmed with love' is actually pretty spot on, but with perhaps a little more emphasis on the 'overwhelmed' and a little less on the 'love' bit. Now, before you lambast me for saying such a wicked thing, this is where we are being totally honest right? The reality is that so many new parents actually don't feel *immediate* bucket loads of love, or sometimes *any* love at all, and that can be absolutely terrifying. Primal instinct to protect and care – yes, most of the time – but overwhelming, gut-wrenching love? Not for everyone – not by a long shot! I know, because, for the first few weeks, that was me. And here's the thing: it is totally and utterly OK, and most importantly, *normal*. Hormones play a big part in this reaction and in chapter 2 I'll be explaining a lot more about them, and what unpredictable beasts they can be.

'Giving birth was a very good experience for me and one I feel truly grateful for. It did, however, become sometimes difficult to tell my story, I felt like I needed to say it was worse than it was in order to stop people from being "jealous". I also didn't cry when I had my daughter, everyone says it's so emotional and you have that connection instantly, I didn't on either count! That worried me slightly.'

Sam, mum to Delilah, aged 13 months

Activity alert

Own it!

This exercise is all about being proud of your birthing experience, whatever it may be, and owning it – a chance for you to really celebrate all you've achieved in becoming a parent and embrace it. Go you!

Fill in the following sentences...

My birthing experience has left me feeling...

The birth of my baby went...

The worst thing about my birth was...

The best thing about my birth was...

I am proud of my birth because...

When I became a parent I felt...

If I could change anything it would be...

I want to congratulate myself and say...

Hopefully you have been kind to yourself and given yourself a great big pat on the back for the incredible job you have done, and continue to do, as a mum or dad.

If for any reason your answers reveal a pattern of sad, negative or anxious feelings, and/or you just don't feel 'right', please don't suffer alone: contact your GP or health visitor for further help and support.

Where is the love? Bonding and hormones

As the Black Eyed Peas once sang, 'Where is the love?' – a question that reverberated round and round my head like a broken record after I had my baby.

I have a diagnosed anxiety disorder, generalised anxiety disorder (GAD), and panic disorder (I've written more about this in my book *Breaking Mad*). I'm lucky in that I normally manage well with my own techniques and medication when needed. However, pregnancy was an increasingly anxious time for me, and in the run-up to delivery day my anxiety levels were gradually building to the point that when I was actually in labour, I swear I was having panic attacks mid-contractions – fun, right?

During contractions, I was so anxious to get the baby out alive, and survive it myself, that I completely forgot all I'd learned in my hypnobirthing classes and basically panicked. Major mistake, but hey, I'm only human and I totally didn't expect contractions (or 'surges' as we were taught – I listened to that bit) to bloody hurt as much as they did from the off. Note to self for next time (IF there's a next time!) – instead of messing about in the classes with the hubby sniggering at the 'how to do perineal massage' video, actually listen and DO the breathing exercises. Everyone experiences pain differently of course, and at differing levels – in fact some mum friends of mine said their labours genuinely didn't hurt – but I was one of the unfortunate sods who had a baby in a back-to-back position pressing down on my sciatic nerve with his head in a seriously unhelpful position – both for him and me.

By the time Enzo was pulled out in a flurry of noise and people bustling around, the last thing I could even begin to fathom was the little puffy-eyed goo-covered creature being shoved in my drowsy face.

Some time later, once I was more with it, my precious bundle was placed in my arms, and I looked down at him ready for the emotion and love to flood out like the crescendo in *The Lion King*'s 'Circle of Life'... and there was... zilch. It was like a car engine had been revving and revving and then at the final moment of go, it stalled.

I stared down at this little person wrapped in towels, sporting a shiner from the forceps that had delivered him, and I can honestly say, at that point, the only emotion I had was pure panic.

'The only way to describe how I felt when I met my baby was absolute shock. There was no gush of overwhelming love that I expected to have. It wasn't until a few months later when my little blob was more like a little person that I realised I loved him more than I ever thought possible.'

Amy, mum to Albie

Instinctively I knew he was mine and that I wanted to keep him safe, but the first thought I had was honestly 'he doesn't look like me'. This cheering thought morphed into an obsession with him being name-tagged, as I didn't want him to be switched with another baby, as happens in horror stories you hear about in the news. Looking back now it's funny the random concerns I had in those first few hours. It was purely primal, but there was no gushing, tear-inducing flood of love – and I was instantly worried. I was *mainly* very worried that something was seriously wrong with me. Why didn't I feel like the love-struck mums in the movies did? Aren't you supposed to blub and coo over your new baby and declare you are 'so so happy' the minute you hold him/her?

I just felt a bit numb if the truth be told. And I know I wasn't alone in feeling that. Of all the new parents I've asked what they felt in the moments after birth (and I bothered lots and lots of them), only ONE said they felt instant love. Wow! I don't know about you, but I found, and find, that a) shocking and b) incredibly comforting...

> *'They decided the safest way forward was to have a Caesarean, which was hugely disappointing, but at this stage an enormous part of me wanted it to be over. All I felt was a bit of rummaging and tugging and then she was here! I was pretty underwhelmed, they showed her to me, and quite honestly I was disappointed she was so squished up and ugly (very un-maternal).'*
>
> **Kim – mum to six-month-old girl**

In the next chapter I'm going to explore how shock and trauma can affect us, and how those pesky hormones can often be responsible for such reactions. I'll also look at the various birth-related mental health conditions that can cause our emotions, feelings and behaviour to go a little haywire JUST when we could really do with them on our side.

If you struggled/or still struggle in any way with your feelings towards your new baby, then you are *not alone*. Our emotions can take one heck of a wallop in those first few hours, days, weeks and months, and I want to reassure you that there are lots of changes, such as hormones, going on in your mind and body that are often responsible for those 'I feel a bit mad' days. Along with the rubbish sleep deprivation, and pressure to be Supermum from the off, it's no wonder our feelings are all over the place! Together, we're going to explore them and work out how to understand the emotional and mental changes being a parent to a newborn brings.

> *'I felt very protective towards our son, but I would be lying if I said I loved him straight away. I was certainly very smitten (and surprisingly maternal!), which definitely helped, but like any relationship, it needed time to develop. There is a very popular adoption saying – "fake it 'til you make it" – and it most definitely helped me in those early days.'*
>
> **Erin, adopted mum to two-year-old Zach**

Dr Reetta says...

The day after birth I'm here to help with understanding what becoming a parent can be like from a psychological perspective. I'm a clinical psychologist, specialising in working with children and parents, and I'm also a mum to two young daughters. My hope is to offer advice and thoughts on the transition to parenthood, with the well-being of both parents and babies in mind.

If you are reading this book while pregnant, your mental well-being is as important at this stage as it is once your baby is here. Do talk to your midwife or another health professional about your emotions. Anxiety in pregnancy is common and research has shown that it is linked to increased likelihood of post-natal depression and anxiety after your baby arrives – so seeking psychological support at this point is something *all* parents-to-be should be encouraged to do, although lots of us still don't.

Anna describes various feelings that are common in new parents following the birth of their baby: shock, surprise, confusion, anxiety and just feeling very emotional. These mixed emotions are very normal, but aren't always talked about.

Becoming a parent for the first time is a significant transition period both for you individually and as a couple, if you are part of one. For women, pregnancy, giving birth and the early days of motherhood are a time of huge change. In the days after your baby arrives you're recovering from giving birth, and getting your head around being a mum. You're probably exhausted, and it might not all be as rosy as you'd imagined! For new dads, the adaptations to fatherhood are also huge, as you come to terms with the changing dynamics in your relationship (there are three of you now), and the shift in roles. Sometimes, in the early days, men can find themselves more in the background, observing, not always knowing how to contribute to everything that is going on around the mother and baby, who are the focus of attention in the hospital, for the midwife, and for friends and family. As a couple you then need to enter a process of 'negotiating' your new roles as parents and transitioning from two to three of you (or more!). Not feeling prepared for this side of things, or expectations not meeting the reality of day-to-day life with a newborn are really common and something I have seen a lot when working with parents.

Top tips for the first few days after birth

1. It is important to acknowledge and remind yourself that emotions in the first few days and weeks of parenthood can be very varied and intense. They can range from exhaustion to irritability, to feeling overwhelmed with love for your baby or with the responsibility that a baby brings. Many new parents are not prepared for these powerful feelings. Perhaps you didn't anticipate the love and closeness you feel towards your baby, and therefore the thought of someone else looking after your baby or you returning to work is unimaginable. Or perhaps the opposite is true, and those feelings aren't flooding in and you're worried about it. Maybe the physical exhaustion is something you have never experienced before, leaving you forgetful and tearful.

2. In the first few weeks and months, make a point of talking to your partner and other parents and exchange stories about the first days and weeks – whether it is old friends with perhaps older children, new friends with new babies going through the same experiences, extended family, your own parents, or random parents you bump into while out and about. Talking and thinking about yourself as a new parent will help you find who you are as a mother or father and get a sense of what you believe in, by comparing and learning from other perspectives. This will help you become stronger in your new identity. Anna's Activity Alerts are a perfect way to get you started when it comes to thinking about your new identity and the journey so far.

3. Whether you had a 'good' or 'bad' birth experience and whether you felt prepared for what it was, you can probably identify with the fact that it involved some level of unpredictability and uncertainty. It sounds like for Anna there was a lot of that! This 'not knowing' is likely to continue throughout the next few months while you settle into new parenthood. Despite all this, parents *do* get through the first months of parenthood – however long it can seem at times. It is important to remember to ask for, and accept, support. 'Not knowing' is a good starting point as it allows some level of flexibility and through 'not knowing' we can *learn*. This will come in handy in the coming months when you are faced with opposing advice from well-meaning family or friends while trying to work out how to help your baby to sleep or feed or do something else 'better'.

2
THE AFTER BIRTH MENTAL STUFF

The 'Who am I?' feeling

IDENTIFICATION CARD

Name: Who am I ?
Issued: a new life
Expires: never

ROLE: NEW PARENT

'
*Being a mother is learning
about strengths you didn't
know you had and dealing with
fears you never knew existed.*
'

Linda Wooten

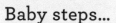

Baby steps...

YOU'VE JUST HAD A BABY. It's a big deal, so it makes sense that you might be feeling all over the place emotionally and mentally. That's absolutely normal, *be kind to yourself* and take each day as it comes.

CONFIDE IN SOMEONE you trust and keep talking through how you're feeling – even if some of the thoughts and feelings are scary and don't make sense, *don't suffer in silence*.

BEING A NEW PARENT is a whole new life change, it can take time to adjust, so allow yourself that time and space to settle into your new role. You're *not alone* and remember – everyone adapts at their own pace.

When hormones kick off

Hormones are a bitch! There, I've said it. I was one of those rather unfortunate people who since the moment puberty started has had unpredictable and very strong hormones. From the day I turned 13 years old it seems, I was cursed with raging premenstrual syndrome (PMS) pretty much most of the time. Each month I'd get a grace period of about a week during which I'd feel chilled and 'me', and then as the wretched hormones ramped up to their 28-day peak I'd be an irritable little madam, susceptible to emotional teenage outbursts (mainly aimed at my parents for 'not getting me'), and moaning about how unfair it was that I was a girl (with the curse) and 'why didn't my brothers have to suffer it too?!'

The irony didn't escape me, even then – as a late developer I'd spent years desperately wanting to fit in with my friends who had already started their periods and I used to look on in envy as they proudly waved their Tampax boxes around in the PE changing rooms, (un)subtly signalling to all that they were now 'officially' a woman. Many a bedtime I'd spend reading Judy Blume's *Are You There, God? It's Me, Margaret* (the 13-year-old girl's bible!) wishing that it was my turn next to join 'The Rag Week Club'. So, the minute my period arrived I did a mental fist pump at no longer being the infantile kid in the changing room in the C&A crop-top training bra. This soon wore off; from the very beginning I *suffered* with my hormones.

Fast forward 20-odd years, after a pregnancy and a new baby had ravaged my body, and my already tetchy hormones were in a whole new league. We had now hit the big time!

But what actually are these hormones and why can they affect our mood, emotions and general sanity at times – particularly when it comes to our baby-making years?

Hormones – breaking them down

Now, I'd just like to clarify that I am no medical expert. You'll find no jargon or scientific paper on the History of Hormones here I'm afraid. But that's actually deliberate – we're too knackered with the broken nights of parenting to have a concentration span of more than a few minutes, right?

Having said that, I've found it hugely beneficial to know just a bit about how my mind and body works and how it was affected during the process of conceiving, carrying and birthing a baby – something that has helped me understand that the feelings of mental fog and total madness at times, particularly during the first few weeks, were due to certain chemical and hormonal changes in my brain.

Hormones are essentially little messages that cause chemical reactions in the brain that then impact the body. Charging around women's bodies during pregnancy, labour and birth in particular (some are always present and play an important role throughout our lives) is a cocktail of these hormones, including oestrogen, progesterone, oxytocin, beta-endorphin and prolactin. These are all very important, and each has their moment to take centre stage before, during and after birth.

For example:

- Oestrogen and progesterone are the champions of your baby-making hormones and play a key role during every stage, not least by helping to maintain increased blood supply for the uterus and breasts during birth.
- Oxytocin helps the body eject the baby by stimulating contractions, and also plays a part in milk production.
- Beta-endorphin acts as a pain killer during labour.
- Prolactin is responsible for milk production and signalling that breastfeeding should kick in.

Pretty cool huh? As you can imagine, these hormones reach fever pitch during the actual birth bit, but what goes up, must come down, and that's pretty much what happens in the aftermath.

After nine months of gearing up for birth day the moment baby is out, our hormones essentially crash out – like they've just won a fight with Mike Tyson – and that can leave us feeling all kinds of crazy weird.

Oxytocin is the big one, and was indirectly the cause of the unwelcome immediate panic and terror I experienced upon being presented with my new baby boy. Why? Because this hormone is responsible for the mother's feelings of attachment, bonding and the protective instinct. It also helps with that all-important let-down reflex that enables the breasts to produce milk. However, it's at this point that it can get a bit tricky and sometimes not quite go to plan – if for example, excess adrenalin caused by a quick or traumatic birth prevents oxytocin from surfacing. Annoyingly, there's nothing we can do about it.

> *'It took me a while to bond with her, I'm not going to lie, I didn't feel that sense of overwhelming love that I was expecting. It took time, and time is the one thing that you can't rush in life, but now I often find myself staring at her – this most remarkable little person, completely challenging and thoroughly gorgeous and brilliant in ways that I never thought imaginable.'*
>
> **Kimberley – mum of four-month-old**

What I didn't know at the time was that as well as all those hormones doing their thing to help a baby to be born, there are also some other chemicals careering around. Adrenalin, for example, is working hard to ensure we're kept safe by switching our bodies into 'fight or flight' mode – that built-in protective mechanism that serves as our little 'panic button' and readies us to either fight the threat, or take flight (flee) from it (more on this in chapter 3).

When hormones go wrong

The Fast Show

SOMETIMES, DURING a very quick labour or when someone has to be induced, the body doesn't get a chance to build up sufficient levels of beta-endorphins to help with the pain and as a result they may experience a more agonising and potentially traumatic birth. This in turn can cause adrenalin levels to remain high for a longer period, blocking the release of oxytocin, and the body may also go into shock for a short while afterwards. As the body recovers, the hormones can gradually start to release.

In my body, my hormones had been dancing the cha cha cha for hours and hours during a long, slow and painful labour, and when at the final hurdle they were faced with the traumatic situation baby and I suddenly found ourselves in, the adrenalin ramped up. This chemical reaction was so intense that it totally obliterated and temporarily over-rode any other hormone – so oxytocin, the love hormone, didn't stand a chance. His name was NOT down, and he was NOT coming in.

So there I was, my baby had finally been delivered safely, he was well, healthy and a respectable 3.28kg (7lb 4oz), and yet I was a shell-shocked, part-paralysed (due to the anaesthesia) zombie. I felt nothing – physically and emotionally. And my God, was I scared. *Why* didn't I feel overwhelming gushing love for this beautiful, much-wanted little boy? Where the hell had all my emotions gone? I stared down at his little squished-up face, his teeny tiny head caked in goo and bearing the marks of a rather forceful forceps delivery, and all I could think of was 'what the hell do I do with him?!'

I'd dreamed for months, years actually, about this moment... And in my vision (I don't mind sharing with you) I'd hold my baby up in front of me in a sunlit room, family all around me, some sort of music crescendo playing, and through a beaming grin I'd weep at the sheer joy of bringing a little being into the world. The harsh reality was like a bucket of ice-cold water had been thrown over my head. I was wired up to all kinds of beeping machines, had a wee bag attached to my nether regions, and was sitting in a windowless hospital recovery theatre – I couldn't even hold my baby due to the sodding wires in my arms. WHY DIDN'T I FEEL HOLLYWOOD MOVIE-STYLE LOVE?!!! What was WRONG with me?

The tears I shed were initially for the sheer disappointment and regret about how my little Enzo came into the world. I remember my dad walking in to see us while I was in this state, and as he cooed over his new grandson, all I could do was burst into exhausted tears and tell him how it had 'all gone wrong'. I was so pissed off – definitely an emotion I hadn't expected to be present.

And here's the thing: no one means to be unfeeling or insensitive, but I lost count of the number of times in the following days and weeks that people would dismiss my shitty birth and simply say 'oh well, at least you have a healthy baby'. Yes *of course* I was grateful that I had a healthy, perfect baby, he really was (and is) the very best, and I felt guilty for moaning as so many others aren't so fortunate, but I was grieving my botched birth and stupid 20-year-old fantasy and it seemed I couldn't talk about it or process it properly. I certainly couldn't switch from knackered, distraught Anna, to happy new mummy Anna, welcoming hordes of visitors for coffee, cake and a coo.

Those first few weeks are a blur, and I'm sad to say not a particularly happy one. Knowing myself as well as I do – and as a therapist myself – I knew that I needed help instantly and at day four post-partum (after birth) I called my friend and consultant psychiatrist Dr Schapira for some much-needed talking therapy and medical intervention to help with the anxiety and terror I was experiencing. I couldn't eat, sleep or smile. I was also extremely concerned about bonding with my son as the oxytocin was well and truly hibernating until it felt the 'danger' had subsided and allowed itself to make an appearance. It was only in week five the love hormone finally decided to come in… and the trigger was my gorgeous boy.

In the meantime I knew I cared about him – I had the instinct to protect and guard him – but I also knew I was ill. I even had a fleeting thought about how the adoption process works and who might be better equipped than me to care for him – a thought that makes me very upset now, as nine months on I couldn't feel more differently. Yet the day he looked up at me on his changing mat and smiled his first smile straight into my face (and I promise you it was NOT wind), was the day it all changed. The feeling of love didn't exactly 'whoosh' at this stage, but looking down at his gummy little smirk, his eyes searching mine, I suddenly felt this warm glow pass through my body, and as I smiled back at him, I involuntarily said out loud 'I love you little one', and the relief at the genuine emotion behind this sentence made me cry (bloody hormones!) – for the first time since his birth – happy tears.

I knew then that things were going to be OK. Not perfect instantly, not by a long shot – I had, after all, a bout of post-natal depression, anxiety and birth trauma to navigate – but the sun was going to shine again, and in that moment I couldn't have been more utterly grateful for, and smitten with, my boy.

> *'I found that I didn't have that instant overwhelming love for the baby after birth that so many people talk about. I obviously loved him and cared for him a lot, but I didn't know the baby yet so it wasn't until I started to know his little quirks and what he liked that the bond really clicked.'*
>
> **Hannah – mum to George, aged 10 months**

It's good to talk

EVERYONE HAS their own birth story, and it's important to process and talk through any thoughts and feelings you have about your own experience. Don't ever feel yours doesn't matter or isn't valid in any way. Whether you have a good or a bad birth, it's life's biggest miracle and it's totally OK *not* to breeze it from the start. I certainly didn't, and the signs were there, waaaaay back in pregnancy days. After all, even before I got pregnant I had a diagnosed and treatable anxiety disorder, so becoming a mum was always going to be a bit of challenge mentally as well as physically.

Understanding mothers' mental health

In this section, we're going to explore some of the more common types of post-natal mental health conditions to watch out for. Particularly if you're pregnant now or thinking about having another child, it's also important to touch on the often less talked-about and well-known prenatal (before birth) conditions, notably antenatal depression (or perinatal depression, as it can also be called). Some people also suffer with a condition called birth phobia, or 'tokophobia' – an extreme fear of being pregnant and of giving birth that goes beyond the normal fear and worry we all feel about birth. For me, knowing about antenatal depression gave me a huge clue about what was potentially to come, and being mindful of it helped me to manage my pregnancy mental health and keep an eye on myself after birth, as best I could.

According to leading UK mental health charity Mind, one in five women are affected by a mental health problem during pregnancy or in the year after giving birth, with the NHS reporting around 1 in 10 women experiencing the most common condition, post-natal depression (PND) – and this figure jumps to 4 in 10 for teenage mums. Mums of multiples are at a slightly higher risk with 1 in 5 at risk of developing PND, and 3 in 10 experiencing post-natal anxiety. Antenatal depression, anxiety and obsessive compulsive disorder (OCD) can happen during pregnancy, and post-natal depression, post-traumatic stress disorder (PTSD), obsessive compulsive disorder and anxiety can kick in after the birth of baby. Antenatal depression and other mental health conditions tend to be less well known and talked about because of the terribly misplaced stigma surrounding them.

We can kind of get our heads around post-natal depression and anxiety in the sense that it's more logical that a new parent will most likely be feeling tired and overwhelmed *after* the birth. However, it's widely presumed that everyone carrying a child is deliriously happy and excited about the impending bundle of joy. The thought that they might be feeling low, anxious or unhappy is hard for some people to comprehend. The thing is, we can feel BOTH these things at the same time, yet it seems to be so taboo for expectant parents – and that includes dads – to dare to admit that they might not always be jumping around for joy at what is to come, and instead are bloody terrified about the unknown – physically, emotionally and mentally.

As I explained earlier, I was always aware that my chances of developing post-natal depression and anxiety were higher than most due to the fact that I have (successfully) managed a diagnosed mental health condition – generalised anxiety disorder and panic disorder – since 2006. The minute I found out I was pregnant (at three weeks) I therefore went to see my GP to discuss how I should manage my mental health during the next nine months as it was recommended I come off my low-dosage anti-anxiety medication (Escitalopram), for the safety of the growing foetus (apparently there's a very low risk of heart-development issues) – a decision that left me feeling a bit vulnerable.

With the supervision of the doctor, I reduced my medication over the course of the following two weeks, until I was no longer taking it. But now I had a niggling worry and fear about the anxiety condition returning, and what it might do to me, and my unborn baby. From the beginning, then, the pressure was on – but mainly in my head. A scary place to be.

With each passing day and week, I would torture myself with thoughts that the baby might be damaged due to any medication still passing through my system. I desperately tried to ignore the nagging voice in my head that taunted me with horrible visions of having an ill baby, a baby that would inherit my mental health issues, a baby that everyone around me was so excited about but that might be in some way 'not perfect' – and in my head, I believed it would all be my fault if I f**ked up the pregnancy and birth bit in any way. The pressure I put on myself was ridiculous, but on the outside I did what most terrified new mums-to-be do, I just swallowed the fear and cracked on with a smile, telling myself to shut up and be grateful for falling pregnant so easily.

Fortunately, knowing what I know and being a counsellor, I recognised a few months in that I *really* wasn't feeling myself any more. I'd had a particularly heated exchange with my poor husband about me not being able to tolerate meat being cooked in the house (another crazy moment that was definitely fuelled by my morning-sickness food aversions... the SMELL of minced beef would make me green) and had promptly burst into hysterical tears – at which point I decided I needed to get some proper help. I just didn't feel right and I had no clue whether this was due to the pregnancy hormones or whether the anxiety disorder was resurfacing – on reflection it was probably both – so I decided to seek some talking therapy to work through my feelings surrounding the pregnancy.

My GP suggested a wonderful lady called Diana who lived near me and who specialised in pregnancy psychology and counselling. The moment I waddled into her therapy room I knew I had made the right choice – a warm, understanding, friendly smile greeted me, and as I sank down into the armchair opposite her, eyeing up the strategically placed tissue box on the coffee table, I wasted no time in grabbing a handful of Kleenex as I let all my irrational fears and thoughts flood out as she listened kindly – bonkers meat-phobia and all!

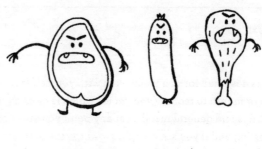

~ meat - phobia ~

The NHS midwifery and antenatal team were also empathetic about my mental health history and would check in with how I was feeling during routine antenatal appointments. Just because I had been signed off 'mentally well' by the consultant, I never felt embarrassed about being honest about how I felt, but there was definitely a niggle in the back of my head that people would think I wasn't able to cope, so I did sometimes pretend to be more 'fine' than perhaps I truly felt. As an anxiety sufferer, this is what lots of us do… we are our own worst enemy at times.

> *'Becoming a mother was more overwhelming than I'd prepared for. During my pregnancy I just assumed "I'm a competent person, I have a high-pressured job, it's one tiny baby – how hard can it be?!" I'm now ashamed of how easily I brushed aside other people's experiences and put myself in another category.'*
>
> **Laura – mum to Saffron**

Being mindful of our mood at all stages of parenthood, before and after, is vitally important in ensuring everyone involved has the best chance of being well, healthy and happy. This next activity can be used to track your mood if you or someone you know is pregnant. You can also give it a go if you're already a parent, to check in on your mood, past and present, to keep yourself as mentally well as possible.

How's your mood?

This activity is designed for you to check in with yourself from week to week or month to month (you decide which is most appropriate) to rate your feelings and general mood. If at any point you are concerned about how you're feeling and if you are creeping towards the bottom of the scale, do contact your health professional for further support and advice. Obviously sleep is entirely dependent on your baby, so try not to judge it based on pre-baby experiences. Instead, focus on what any sleep you do manage to get is like.

Using a scale of 1–10 (1 being the lowest/bad and 10 the highest/good), answer each of these questions as honestly as you can about how you're feeling:

During the last week would you say you've been feeling more down than usual?

How would rate your ability to fall/stay asleep (until a certain someone decides they need attention)?

How would rate your quality of sleep? (We're not expecting any 10s here!)

Have you been feeling more irritable than usual?

Any feelings of restlessness and/or lack of satisfaction?

Have you had any upsetting thoughts?

Do you want to, and are you able to, carry out your usual everyday activities, eg washing, dressing, eating?

Are you mostly enjoying your day to day activities? (nappy changing aside!)

How would you rate your interest in doing things and seeing people?

Overall, rate your current mood out of 10?

Keep checking in with your mood scale to assess yourself. It might even be helpful to talk through your findings with your GP or health professional in order for them to help support you.

A darker shade of baby blues

You've probably heard of the baby blues – a phenomenon that's widely talked about in parenting circles and is an accepted part of the childbirth journey. Indeed, 50–70 per cent of us experience them shortly after birth. Usually this coincides with day three, when the milk starts coming in and those hormones are yo-yoing as you come down from the adrenalin high of the birth, though it can catch some of us out a few weeks later. Dads can also feel a degree of these 'blues' as their emotions have most likely taken a battering, too. Generally, they shouldn't last longer than a few weeks.

If you do get a case of the blues you might find yourself crying for no apparent reason, feeling utterly exhausted and perhaps not quite as elated and excited as hoped. Feelings of being overwhelmed and that it's all a bit of an anticlimax are all pretty common during this time – remember, this is *completely normal*. It does NOT mean you're a crap mother – which doesn't stop lots of us worrying about exactly that in those early days.

I clearly remember sitting (gingerly, on a cushion) on my sofa a few days after having Enzo. We had just come home from hospital where I basically hadn't slept for five days, having been kept in for three nights after the two-day labour due to severe anaemia and generally feeling weak and wobbly (wow, those post-labour wards are noisy huh?), and for no apparent reason at all I burst into tears and started wailing like a child, doing those hiccup-y sobs that toddlers do when they've fallen over and hurt themselves. Thankfully, my husband was on hand to give me a much-needed cuddle, a cup of tea, and to put *Strictly* on the telly to cheer me up.

Now, usual baby blues generally clear up and ease off after a few days, or a week or two. It's when these feelings hang around like an unwanted smell for just that little bit too long, and even start to develop into slightly more intense feelings that we need to be careful. It can be hard to admit to yourself, let alone anyone else, that you're not feeling that great, but it's vitally important a) not to suffer in silence hoping it will just pass, and b) to get help and support – there is plenty out there if you ask for it – from your GP, health visitor and community midwives, all of whom can support you by offering coping suggestions, talking therapies and even medication if needed. Know that this does NOT make you a bad mum or dad – in fact it makes you an incredibly *brave* and *sensible* one. Taking note of and nipping in the bud any early niggles is essential in making sure nothing more sinister is brewing.

If your perfectly natural baby blues don't seem to be shifting, or are getting worse – and perhaps are being added to with other thoughts, feelings, behaviours and fears – then it's definitely worth seeking some further help. I know from my own experience that it can feel scary and daunting to admit that you're not bathing in the warm glow of motherhood but actually feeling pretty shitty, and there is no shame or embarrassment in asking for a helping hand.

There are a few more serious conditions that are a step up from the usual baby blues. If any of the ones I mention below resonate with you it's definitely time to reach out by giving your medical professionals a call and also finding a trusted partner, family member or friend to confide in. This is not the time to suffer in silence.

'Lots of new mums (like me) unexpectedly find themselves in that rather grey area that no one talks about between the baby blues and a diagnosis of post-natal anxiety or depression. I found it really hard to move overnight from doing a demanding and fulfilling professional job, in which I felt very capable and confident, to struggling haplessly with a newborn baby.'

Lyn – mum to an IVF baby girl

Breaking it down

Post-natal depression (PND)

This is perhaps the most widely known post-birth mental health illness, yet one that unfairly still carries huge stigma. Nobody asks to have PND and I think the embarrassment and shame surrounding it is due to the fact we don't feel like we *should* be 'depressed' in any way – after all we've just created a lovely little baby and have lots of nice presents to be excited about. It doesn't help when well-meaning friends and family offer up statements such as 'you must be so happy', and 'I bet you're on cloud nine aren't you?' For those experiencing PND, no we're not on cloud nine thank you very much, we're right down in the dumps – and we can't help it or 'pull ourselves together'.

Post-natal depression can occur at any time during that first year post delivery and affects around 1 in 10 mothers (excluding teenagers and mothers of multiples, for whom the statistic is higher). It can also affect fathers and partners, although this is less common. Symptoms include:

- a persistent feeling of sadness and low mood;
- lack of enjoyment and loss of interest in the wider world;
- feeling detached from life in general;
- lack of energy and feeling tired all the time;
- trouble sleeping at night and feeling sleepy during the day;

- difficulty bonding with your baby;
- withdrawing from contact with other people;
- problems concentrating and making decisions;
- grieving for your 'old life' pre baby;
- disturbing or frightening thoughts, such as hurting yourself or baby.

Lots of people don't realise they're experiencing PND as it can develop gradually, but being aware of how you're feeling, and not dismissing prolonged feelings of any of the above, and getting help as soon as possible is key to maintaining healthy mental and emotional well-being. You're not going mad, your baby won't be taken away from you, so be brave and ask for support. In chapter 9 I'll be shedding some more light on what to expect, and the options available to you when medical professionals are on hand to help.

> 'He was a surprise baby conceived not long after losing another baby mid term, so all of my grief seemed to surface at this point. I did not have time to properly grieve the baby I had lost. The moment I was home from hospital a huge wave of sadness hit me and it took about four weeks to pass – I was in a sad and introverted mood for some time.'
>
> **Melissa – mum of four**

Birth trauma and post-traumatic stress disorder (PTSD)

According to the Birth Trauma Association, in the UK alone as many as 200,000 women each year experience birth trauma following a traumatic birth, and of these, 1 in 10 will go on to develop PTSD as a result of their experience.

Birth trauma and PTSD is essentially the same thing. The terms relate to women who have developed extreme psychological distress as a consequence of their experiences during childbirth. They may have had severe complications, undergone medical interventions without pain relief, and in some tragic cases, stillbirth. Other women may have had a relatively 'normal' birth but are also severely affected by other things, such as loss of control, loss of dignity or negative attitudes of others around them at the time. Some commonly reported reasons for developing post-birth PTSD include:

- lengthy labour or short and very painful labour;
- being induced;
- poor pain relief;
- feelings of loss of control;
- high levels of medical intervention;
- traumatic or emergency deliveries, eg emergency caesarean section;
- impersonal treatment or problems with the staff attitudes;
- not being listened to;
- lack of information or explanation;
- lack of privacy and dignity;
- a sudden birth with limited medical help – such as an unanticipated home birth;
- an unexpected, or shock, birth – premature, or didn't know was pregnant;
- fear for baby's safety;
- an experience involving the threat of death or serious injury to either you or another person close to you (eg your baby)
- birth of a damaged baby (a disability resulting from birth trauma);
- baby's stay in intensive care;
- poor post-natal care;
- previous trauma (for example, in childhood, or with a previous birth).

Some women (and dads and partners) may experience *some* of these feelings but not all.

You may have heard of PTSD in relation to other situations, such as military combat, terrorist attacks or serious accidents or incidents. Essentially the term means a set of normal reactions to a traumatic, scary or bad experience and has in recent years also been included as a condition experienced by those who have had traumatic births.

Characteristics of birth trauma and PTSD can include:

- A response of intense fear (such as panic attacks), helplessness or horror to that experience.

- The persistent re-experiencing of the event by way of recurrent intrusive memories, flashbacks and nightmares. You feel distressed, anxious or panicky when exposed to things that remind you of the event.
- Avoidance of anything that reminds you of the trauma. This can include talking about it, although sometimes women may go through a stage of discussing their traumatic experience a lot so that it obsesses them at times – which is also not healthy.

Sufferers might have difficulties with sleeping and concentrating. You may also feel angry, irritable and be hyper vigilant (feel jumpy or on your guard all the time). It's also very possible for the new dad or partner to experience symptoms of birth trauma and PTSD if they've perhaps witnessed a troubling birth – I know my husband felt traumatised for a while after seeing his wife and baby in such distress, as for a brief moment, he feared the worst.

If you or someone you know is experiencing birth trauma and PTSD then do contact your local GP, health visitor or midwife for help and support. Counselling and psychotherapy can be hugely beneficial in working through the experience. It might also be useful to contact the hospital or birthing unit you birthed at or with (if a home birth) to book a birth reflection session. You can also choose to seek your own therapist if you prefer. Have a look at the resources section at the back of the book.

'I also suffered panic attacks almost every day for the first few weeks and would lie in bed wide awake while the baby was fast asleep sweating and shaking violently. I felt so much guilt as I looked at this beautiful, perfect little baby that I was so excited to meet, because all I thought now was "what on earth have we done?"'

Amy – mum to Alfie, aged 10 months

Post-natal anxiety (PNA) and obsessive compulsive disorder (OCD)

PNA and OCD are being increasingly talked about, as they're becoming more understood – feeling anxious is a normal reaction to becoming a parent and PNA and OCD are issues new mums in particular should be mindful of. The physical shock of giving birth, mixed with hormone fluctuations, disrupted sleep, stress levels and the general life change that having a new baby can cause results in almost 1 in 10 mothers worldwide experiencing the terrifying feelings that come hand in hand with PNA and OCD.

Those suffering will often be feeling panicky, fearful, worried, and combating obtrusive, frightening thoughts, such as 'what if I drop the baby down the stairs?' or 'what if my baby dies in the night?' These thoughts and feelings are thought to be caused by the hormonal changes that take place during pregnancy and birth, and the stress of giving birth.

Typical symptoms include:

- obsessive, intrusive thoughts that keep popping into your mind;
- feeling scared all the time;
- not wanting to leave the house or avoiding certain places;
- panic attacks;
- insomnia;
- compulsive behaviour, such as checking or doing things in a specific routine;
- constantly thinking about worst-case scenarios;
- lack of appetite.

Keep track of how you're feeling post birth – and also during your pregnancy if you're at that stage – and if any of these feelings are ringing true with you, do contact your health professionals for advice, help and support. It's important, too, to confide in a trusted pal or partner as it can really help lighten the load (and anxiety).

> *'I try to be positive and*
> *put on a brave face and a number*
> *of people have said they can't believe how*
> *well I look after having my babies but they don't*
> *realise how awful I feel, and the fact I've lost my*
> *baby weight so quickly is because I've been*
> *too anxious to eat sometimes.'*
>
> **Mum of twins**

Postpartum psychosis (PP)

You may have seen this particularly severe strain of motherhood mental health illness on sensationalist TV shows such as *EastEnders*, where recently one of the characters, with an already diagnosed mental health issue (bipolar disorder), developed postpartum psychosis after having her baby. The character displayed hallucinations and worrying, disturbing thoughts and was eventually admitted to a specialist mother-and-baby unit for help, which is certainly the best place for immediate care, medication and support for a suffering mum, however there might be an initial period of separation for mum to get the help and medication she needs in order to care for herself and baby sufficiently.

Postpartum psychosis (PP) is a rare (about 1 in 1000 pregnancies), severe, but treatable, form of mental illness that can occur after having a baby. It can more commonly affect women with a history of previous mental illness, particularly those with bipolar disorder, but it can also happen out of the blue to women without previous experience of mental illness. PP normally begins in the first few days to weeks after childbirth. It can get worse very quickly and should always be treated as a medical emergency.

These are some of the symptoms that women with postpartum psychosis can experience:

- feeling excited, elated, or 'high';
- feeling depressed, anxious, or confused;
- feeling excessively irritable or changeable in mood;
- strange beliefs that could not be true (delusions);

- hearing, seeing, feeling or smelling things that are not there (hallucinations);
- high mood with loss of touch with reality (mania);
- severe confusion;
- being more talkative, sociable, on the phone an excessive amount;
- a very busy mind or racing thoughts;
- feeling very energetic and like 'Supermum' or agitated and restless;
- trouble sleeping, or not feeling the need to sleep;
- behaving in a way that is out of character or out of control;
- feeling paranoid or suspicious of people's motives;
- feeling that things are connected in special ways or that stories on the TV or radio have special personal meaning;
- feeling that the baby is connected to God or the Devil in some way.

The main thing to remember is that as scary as postpartum psychosis can be for the sufferer, as well as the surrounding loved ones, it IS treatable and with the right intervention and treatment you WILL make a recovery. It might take some time but women do return to their normal selves and pick up being 'mummy' again.

It's also worth reassuring you that there is no evidence to suggest that a baby's long-term development is affected by PP. Above all, it is critical that you GET HELP immediately if any of the above apply.

Help is at hand

IT'S SO important not to bottle things up and struggle on in silence hoping that the baby fog will just lift or disappear. There's every chance it might, but it's also important to remember that you don't have to be Mary Poppins and 'practically perfect in every way' (and she wasn't even a mum – she got to hand back the reins!). There is loads of help and empathy out there (me for one) that can ease or lift that mental burden from you.

YOUR GP, HEALTH VISITOR, community midwife, hospital maternity department, and charities and organisations such as the NCT, Mind, PANDAS Foundation, The Birth Trauma Association, The APP Network and Anxiety UK are all full of guidance and reassurance. You'll find all the details at the back of the book.

Dr Reetta says...

After birth mental well-being As Anna notes,
mental health problems during pregnancy or in the first year after giving birth are reasonably common. Anna has helpfully outlined the diagnostic labels covering all post-natal distress. The most often talked about label is post-natal depression (PND), which is sometimes used as a bit of a catch-all category, as it is the best-researched area of post-natal distress in women.

It's useful to think about post-natal distress on a sliding scale, rather than something that you either 'have' or 'do not have' – most parents have days when they could tick the boxes for being depressed or anxious! Parents who don't experience extreme distress needing a diagnosis are still going through a significant transformation psychologically.

In trying to understand our mental health after birth, it's important to keep in mind psychological, social and cultural factors – in addition to the hormonal factors Anna has been talking about. There are a number of psychological theories about why new parents experience post-natal distress. These include the unrealistic expectations of parenthood, which can then cause perfectionist and controlling tendencies, leading to anxiety and low mood. Consider the media stories and images of a new mother: nurturing, sexy, glowing, hair perfect, and unfazed by day-to-day challenges of breastfeeding, sleep deprivation and household chores. This Supermum is a fiction – and one of the reasons why many women feel inadequate when they aim for such unachievable perfection.

New mums also often report that they don't have any time to do things they enjoy any more, and also that they don't have any control over their lives – the baby takes over. A lack of role models and support networks as people often live further from their extended family can also make parents feel out of control and unable to cope with all their new responsibilities. There can be complex choices around family and work, too, when women have built their careers before having children – it is always tough balancing everyone's needs. All these factors together can help us better understand why so many parents experience post-natal distress.

Top tips for looking after your mental health

1. Educate yourself about the symptoms of post-natal mental health difficulties (Anna's chapter covers it all). Then keep an eye on your mood and anxiety levels – you can do it by using Anna's 'How's your mood?' Activity Alert. As Anna says, asking for help does *not* make you a bad parent. It actually communicates something quite useful to your baby: 'it's OK to ask for support', 'it's important to look after yourself', and 'it's OK to talk about not feeling OK'. These messages will be useful as your baby grows older and learns to regulate their own emotions.

2. Were there any traumatic aspects of the birth process? The lack of control that many women and men experience (we like and are used to feeling in control), as well as any trauma can stay with you. You may or may not be healed physically, but are there any psychological wounds of giving birth that feel raw? If you have difficult memories about the birth and these pop up and upset you daily, it's helpful to face them and deal with them. The idea is that if you 'process' a traumatic memory, it is less likely to 'stay with you' and negatively impact on you as you go forwards. You may want to do this with a professional and think about what the difficult aspects meant to *you* or *about* you.

3. Find one simple thing to do for *yourself* each day. For many parents, this is very difficult (or almost impossible!) in the early days, especially if you have older children, but have a think: is there a 10-minute window in which you could focus on yourself? Of course there will always be other things that have to be done, but for a couple of moments each day, put yourself first. Make sure to include lots of realistic activities that can be done while you are with your baby, such as deep breathing, talking to another parent, listening to something you have specifically chosen on the radio. If you are already doing this, do you notice and appreciate those moments? Think of these as your 'self-care moments' – as necessary in your daily routine as changing a nappy or getting your baby to sleep – but these are about you and looking after your mental health.

Moments of mindfulness

Build quick moments of mindfulness into your day while feeding your baby. Whether you are sitting down to give a bottle, breastfeed, or pump, use some of this time to centre yourself and be 'here and now'. Breathe in through your nose and out through your mouth, slow and deep – repeat three times. Focus on that moment through your senses and think of three things you can hear (eg your baby's breath, traffic or the washing machine), see (eg your baby's face, a coffee cup or a pile of laundry) and feel (eg your baby's skin, the floor under your feet or the chair you are sitting on). When you get distracted, bring your focus back to your breath. Continue with this exercise for 3–5 minutes and note how you feel afterwards.

Another time when mindfulness can help new parents is when your baby is crying for long periods of time. Notice your thoughts and feelings as you attend to your baby. Think of a calming mantra you can say to yourself, such as, 'this is not an emergency', 'this is not a catastrophe' or, 'I'm doing everything I can to soothe my baby'. Keep bringing your attention to the present moment, while also focusing on breathing deeply and calmly, as you carry on soothing, attending to and holding your baby.

3
THE AFTER BIRTH PHYSICAL STUFF

The 'run over by a truck' feeling

'*I'm not finding pregnancy much of a joy. I am afraid of childbirth, but I am afraid I can't find a way of avoiding it.*'

Bridget Bardot

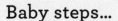

Baby steps...

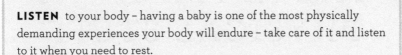

LISTEN to your body – having a baby is one of the most physically demanding experiences your body will endure – take care of it and listen to it when you need to rest.

TIME is a healer – never a truer saying than when recovering from childbirth. You may feel broken in the early aftermath, but you WILL feel better physically as Mother Nature helps repair and restore your body.

DON'T MEASURE yourself against anyone else's recovery – just because so and so is already signing up for Buggy Fit moments after giving birth, it doesn't mean you have to compete. Go at your own pace.

> * Warning: if you are yet to experience the 'joy' of childbirth and are in a blissful pre-birth bubble and would rather stay there, thank you very much, it's going to get pretty graphic so you might want to skip this chapter and come back once you're through the other side.*

Let's get physical

I have ummed and ahhed a lot about what to include in this chapter. It has in fact become quite the discussion point among my friends and colleagues, most of whom are mothers, or about to become one, with regards to how much detail to go into when it comes to the nitty gritty of childbirth. I do believe it's not for anyone to project their experiences on to another person, unless it's been asked for by the receiver. Everyone has a unique birth and the very last thing I want to do is to evoke even a smidgeon of anxiety or fear in an expectant mum – that would be foolish and irresponsible of me in a book that's about tackling anxiety!

However, having thought long and hard about how much to open up to you and tell you how it was for me, and after gaining a lot of feedback from mum pals, the majority have reasoned that they wish they had known much more *beforehand* about how birth can feel as, like me, they went into the whole labour process thinking that breathing and panting would suffice (and it did for some of them, fear not!). The harsh reality for many mums, though, was that it was a pretty challenging ordeal that hurt a lot more than they thought it would. Not being any the wiser they felt like they in some way failed, were crap at giving birth, and generally as though they should have coped better. A lot of these mums developed feelings of low self-esteem and anxiety as a result. Hindsight is of course a wonderful thing, but after much discussion, lots of the new mums and pregnant women I interviewed asked me to include this chapter in the fairly graphic way I have, so at least for those who might want to have an insight into a fairly bad birth, it's here for the taking.

On the flip side, some mums told me they went through pregnancy deliberately ignoring TV programmes such as *One Born Every Minute* and not reading a thing as they preferred to just go with the flow or were too anxious to want to know. Some mothers feel very strongly that no mother-to-be should hear anything remotely negative about birth, and others have implored me to share my, and others' stories in order to feel normal, less lonely, and more positive about their own experiences. *All* agree that anyone who is slightly fearful, prone to anxiety, or would rather just leave things to Mother Nature – and in one mum's words 'float through pregnancy in a state of blissful ignorance' – would perhaps be better just skipping over this chapter.

The main thing is you take care of yourself, and know what you need and want to hear, emotionally and mentally.

Getting real

I don't care how much the books and magazine articles dress it up with 'you soon forget the pain', and the 'it's so worth it' nonsense – unless you're somehow void of all sensation (and there are also just some women who genuinely don't find giving birth painful), the fact is that for most of us, giving birth doesn't half sting. A lot. In fact, thinking about it, pregnancy can smart a bit, too, what with the sore boobs, stretching ligaments, frequently being winded by baby kicks to the ribcage and, if you're part of the 'Farmer Giles' club like me, embracing the joys of pregnancy piles (haemorrhoids) – it's safe to say that few come through the whole experience unscathed.

So, before we delve in, I must once again remind you that a lot of this is my opinion, I didn't enjoy giving birth – there, I said it. But lots of friends and new mums tell me how much they embraced giving birth, found it empowering, and I've had more than one new mum tell me they felt like Superwoman and as though they could conquer the world straight after giving birth – they found the whole experience liberating. And let's be honest, what we consider painful varies from person to person. My pain threshold is low. So low in fact that I had a general anaesthetic once to take a tooth out. To say I'm hardcore would be a complete lie, so I do appreciate that my perspective on this chapter is merely that, my perspective, and should be treated as one person's experience, in order to gain some sort of insight into a warts-and-all birth account, and to alleviate any nagging feelings of post-birth anxiety and low mood.

This chapter is all about being honest, open and real about some of the gorier and frequently embarrassing aspects of childbirth, namely the physical stuff. The stuff that impacts how we feel about giving birth and informs our unique opinion. Women have been giving birth since the dawn of time – it's a commonplace event: births happen all over the world every minute of the day. However, that doesn't, and more importantly *shouldn't*, take away from each woman's individual experience. It shouldn't ever detract from *your* experience. I've lost count of the amount of times new mothers brush their discomfort, pain and exhaustion under the carpet, embarrassed by society into not wanting to make a fuss as 'everyone else does it so I should just suck it up too'. WRONG!

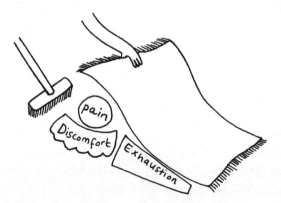

Just because gazillions of people pop sprogs out, admittedly some with more ease than others, it doesn't mean we can't moan about and debrief our own experiences – in fact, quite the opposite, it's helpful to do just that. In chapter 9 I'm going to talk even more about how we can do this professionally with a birth reflection.

Now remember, this is a book about parenting anxiety and mental health, and just because some women have non-complicated births, it doesn't mean for one moment that their feelings and emotional state after they've experienced childbirth aren't equally important. Even if their privates are wonderfully intact, it doesn't mean that other physical and mental issues can't arise and be as upsetting and traumatic as those experienced by people who had more traumatic births. Remember girls, we all experience our own highs and lows at different points during our birthing journey. We all have a voice that deserves to be listened to.

> *'After a quick birth, I was concerned I wasn't healing well – it took some time and was probably made worse by the amount of walking I did in the first weeks. I wasn't sure how I would cope with so much time indoors and without much structure to the days so I compensated by getting out A LOT. I still think this was the right approach for me.'*
>
> **Steph – mum to Livy, aged 10 months**

The final push

It's cosy in here!

Most new parents can talk of little else. You only have to be a fly on the wall in a baby weigh-in clinic or an NCT coffee club to hear tales of episiotomies, forceps and emergency C-sections as new mums jostle to share their birth stories, desperate for an empathetic ear. It's like Birth Story Bingo. You hit the jackpot when you stumble across someone else who has encountered a similar experience, and with a knowing look of sympathy you instantly connect over your shared knackered baby-making bits, or whatever. I remember seeing two women, strangers, actually embrace in a drop-in clinic's toilets after sharing a passing quip about their lax pelvic floor.

In my haste to offload my own tale of woe, I remember not even being able to wait until the more appropriate audience of a baby group, and ended up prattling on to some poor woman in the supermarket check-out queue as I was bulk buying formula, about how 'bloody awful' my experience was, and how I couldn't sit down properly without the aid of a cushion wedged up my arse. Said woman politely smiled and nervously laughed as though I was joking (I wasn't). Instead she did what everyone does when they don't want to hear the (admittedly rather too candid) truth, she ignored the awkwardness and instead coochy cooed my boy snuggled up in his pram – trying her best to ignore the oversized matching tracksuit- and flip-flop*-wearing weirdo (me) standing next to her.

(* It was October and as my feet were still swollen with fluid retention the only shoes that fit were my flip-flops.)

And this is the thing: few people (bar other new mums) want to hear the crap bits about your birth. Quite understandably, they just want to gush over your new little baby, but the more disregarded our experience and feelings, the more it can weigh us down with unresolved emotions, perhaps of regret, resentment or confusion about how the birth ended. It can also leave us feeling anxious, stressed and upset. As is the case in a lot of situations we encounter in life, if we harbour feelings of negativity or upset, we often can't move forwards properly until someone gives us the chance to offload those feelings. When giving birth takes a different path to what we've perhaps planned, prepared or hoped for, it can be utterly terrifying, a massive let-down, and can be in large part responsible for us mums experiencing all kinds of emotionally and mentally challenging feelings afterwards.

My birth story

> **WARNING!** If you do **NOT** wish to delve into other people's birth stories, I recommend you skip this next bit.

As you've probably gathered by now, my birthing experience was an A-grade shit-fest. From the moment I went a day overdue I became an even more anxious tetchy vat of hormones waiting to go off like a bomb at any minute. My darling son chose to hang on in there for a full 10 DAYS longer than we had hoped, and when I finally woke at 5am on the Monday morning to the first scary, yet exciting, twinges of early labour, I foolishly thought 'great, gimme a few hours and I'll have a baby'. The next bit I've decided to include in order to share and offer empathy and support to others, not evoke fear! Remember, this was MY birth, and yours will be, or has been, completely unique to you.

So here it is, my warts-and-all 40 hours or so of giving birth.

5am – Electric shock-like pains in my lower back every 10 minutes. Wake husband, stick the Tens machine on and have a cuppa. We are both like kids on Christmas Day timing the 'surges' (hypnobirthing lingo for contractions) and generally faffing about with pillows, birthing balls, soothing music etc.

Noon – Pains are increasing in my back – where are the lower frontal period pains I've been anticipating? What's this back pain bollocks about? No one told me about this?! Order hubby to ring the labour ward, who demand to speak to me to see if I'm *really* in labour. I fail the test and am told to stay at home until contractions are '3 in 10' (three contractions in every 10 minutes).

4pm – Basically lie, ring the hospital again and say contractions are '3 in 10' as I'm bored and impatient at home and want some pain relief – the Tens machine ain't cutting it and the back pain is getting really rather bad now.

5pm – Waddle into the birthing unit, snack bag, new pillow and bedraggled husband in tow. Get shown into lovely bright and airy birthing room containing a pool (yes!)... We are IN.

5.15pm – And we are OUT. Silly midwife says I'm only 1cm (1/2in) dilated and have to go home. I start crying and swearing.

8pm – Back pains are off the scale in intensity. Still no period-pain-like contractions: it turns out I'm 'back labouring' like my Mum did and baby is likely to be pressing on my spinal nerve, hence the relentless pain. OH JOY!!! Again, why did nobody ever tell me about 'back-to-back labour'?! (See the box below, FYI.)

1 cm

a cheerio

10pm – Scream at (laptop-surfing) husband for asking me 'what type of broadband should we switch to?' as I bend over the kitchen table feeling like some knife-wielding masochist is plunging a blade into my lower back every two minutes. Husband announces he's 'a bit bored', I lose my shit. Big time.

Midnight – A saviour arrives! My mother (having been called in as reinforcement by verbally-abused hubby) takes charge. Sends the other half off to bed to rest and to stop antagonising me, and sets up a 'contraction camp' with birthing ball, six pillows and her very adept hand to rub my back.

1am – I CAN'T DO THIS!!!!! The time for hypnobirthing bullshit is no more. Mum and hubby race me to hospital (again), where upon arrival I simultaneously wet myself and projectile vomit in front of the ward's automatic doors.

1.05am – Cry pathetically to a lovely kindly midwife who, by way of torture, due to me needing monitoring, an IV drip due to severe dehydration, and potential hardcore drugs due to back-to-back baby – leads us straight through the tranquil birthing unit and into the hardcore consultant-led labour ward. Shit just got real.

1.30–7am – Not quite sure what the hell happened in this time vortex but apparently I yelled – a lot – ingested a shed load of diamorphine, gas and air and some other drugs – can't really remember what – accidentally kicked a midwife in the face mid-examination, went a bit crazy and in a drug-induced stupor slurred to my birthing team that 'this was MY show and I was the star, so they could all f**k off' – how classy.

7am – I'm tired and still not really progressing. I beg for an epidural. And am kindly reminded that it 'says in my birth plan I wanted to go as natural as possible...' The subsequent response cannot be printed in this book due to its expletive nature, but suffice it to say that 20 minutes later the anaesthetist walked in and ordered me to 'sit up on the bed and lean forwards'.

7.30am – Oh the lovely lovely lovely drugs. Epidurals are pain-relief heaven, molten liquid pain-relief gold hitting the spot perfectly – and I didn't feel a thing when he injected it. With all pain finally numbed and feeling a little bit more relaxed, I set about apologising to the birthing professionals I've just sworn at for the past six hours straight.

7.30am–4pm – I coast along in a haze of epidural bliss, try to have a snooze – can't – eat a ham sandwich and a bag of Jelly Babies. Medical people keep coming in and checking me and baby. Progress is slow, baby is in an odd position and still back to back. Hormone-induction drip is administered, waters are broken by midwife, contractions are ramping up – finally. Don't really feel anything due to lovely pain relief.

4pm – I'm 10cm (4in) dilated – the Holy Grail! I can start pushing. Get on to all fours on bed, not an easy feat as half my body is semi-paralysed with the epidural, but give it a go assisted by mum, husband and lovely midwife. Push like the clappers cheered on by hubby who puts on the *Rocky IV* theme tune for 'inspiration'.

a BAGEL

5.30pm – Houston there seems to be a problem! A BIG ASS problem. Baby is stuck. Lots of strangers in white coats rush in, it seems there's a queue of people waiting to stick their hands up my vag and have a rummage around... It is declared I can 'do no more' and the medical team now need to 'get baby out pronto!'

6–7pm – The worst 'best' hour of my life. Terrified, dazed, exhausted and already majorly sleep deprived, I get wheeled into theatre to be greeted by 20 or so doctor people all gowned up and ready for battle. I cry (again), husband looks equally terrified (but also quite fit in his ER scrubs), I sign lots of bits of paper to allow 'procedures' to happen, repeat my name and date of birth a zillion times, and get asked umpteen times if I 'understand' what's about to happen (of course I bloody don't, but I say yes).

I sit up on the bed and lean forwards (again) for another epidural... then a spinal block to ensure I'm really numb below the chest... get put in position, legs akimbo and in stirrups, and catch a glimpse of the forceps that are about to help the baby out!

'When I say push, PUSH!' Things go rather hazy, the anaesthetic double whammy has more than done its job, perhaps a little too well as I start to feel rather sleepy... I hear my husband say in earnest 'come on Anna, PUSH!' I hear the best sound in the world... a baby cry... and my hubby tearfully whispering to me, 'Anna we've had a little boy'. Then I see the flash of a mushed-up goo-covered face staring up into mine from my chest, before my 30-seconds-old son is taken away to be cleaned up while I basically fall asleep with the exhaustion and shock of it all.

After 40 hours of labouring, I came out of it all alive, if not completely unscathed – I had a reasonably impressive post-partum haemorrhage (lost some blood), an episiotomy, and a forceps delivery. Although I felt as though I'd been run over by a truck, then reversed over a few more times for good measure, I was alive, well (ish), and more importantly, so was my beautiful new son.

OK – now I hope I haven't been too graphic or put the fear into anyone. I've thought long and hard about including this description in this book – my very last intention is to cause anyone unnecessary anxiety about giving birth. But I also think the object of this book is to be honest and open, with the aim of being helpful, empathetic and helpful. From the feedback I've had, I feel I owe it to you to not be another hushed-into-silence new mother, and instead throw caution to the wind and include my experience with the sole aim of providing comfort to the many others who tell me they also felt, and feel, the same.

So many people tell me they also had scary moments and yet have felt compelled to keep shtum for fear of upsetting others (and I get that, no one wants to intentionally worry another mum or dad), so with great trepidation, I'm being as real as I dare about my birthing experience, as how I dealt with it is hugely connected to the emotional and mental health fall-out that happened in those early days, weeks and months.

I would also like to reassure you that during my son's birth, no matter how scary it felt at the time, I was safe, under expert care, and physically recovered well and quickly – quite miraculously actually. The NHS and its medical and midwifery team are a credit to us all and I am in forever in their debt.

Birthing the afterbirth

Once the anaesthetic had worn off I remember thinking to myself 'holy crap, what has my body just endured?!' On one hand I was proud and in awe that my little 5ft 3in self had managed to achieve the mammoth task of actually getting a real life baby out of it, but on the other I was in a state of shock, sporting a rather fetching pair of surgical socks and unable to feel my lower half.

The fact is, though, that labour doesn't end when the baby has popped out – there's still the placenta to deliver, and the afterpains as your uterus contracts, and how these feel and how well the process goes can greatly vary. One mum told me her story of sitting up in bed with her nightie rucked up around her hips, trying to get her minutes-old baby to breastfeed while she entered the third stage of labour (the delivery of the placenta), which, once the contractions had resumed, felt like she was giving birth all over again. Other mums say they never noticed the placenta 'birth' bit, but some speak of it quite poignantly. Either way, it's an incredibly important phase since if the placenta refuses to come out or is partially retained then infection can set in and haemorrhaging can occur.

Then there's also the contracting of the uterus that happens soon after birth. I felt a bit squeamish as it gradually shrank down over several days, but didn't find it particularly painful, whereas some mothers, particularly those who have had more than one child, say it's a whole new pain-relief ball game in itself enduring the uterine contractions, since it usually happens much more rapidly for subsequent births.

Assisted births – when you need some extra help

Nope, I'm not ready!

There has been a bit of a frankly long-overdue shift in the news and media recently around natural versus assisted births. For a long time there has been a pressure, propaganda almost, that natural births are 'best', but thankfully these opinions and campaigns are being increasingly shelved in order to stop women feeling like failures if they don't, or can't, go down this route. Every birth is deserving of the same level of respect and praise and yet lots of women say they've somehow been made to feel rubbish, less of a woman even, if they've had anything other than a natural birth. Which is terrible! Let me tell you, there is nothing 'less' about having any sort of procedure to ensure the delivery of a healthy baby!

Intervention or assisted births are when mum and baby need a helping hand, and according to the Royal College of Obstetricians and Gynaecologists account for almost one in eight (12 per cent) of vaginal births in the UK, and for Caesarians it's around one in every four.

There are several reasons why the decision to intervene by doctors and midwives is taken. These can include the baby being overdue (or it being safer for mum and baby if the baby is born early), in distress or showing a reduced heart rate; the baby being in an awkward position; the waters having broken but contractions not starting; and/or the mother being too tired to carry on without some extra help.

It can be hugely daunting and frightening for an expectant mother to be told she needs a helping hand to have her baby. It can also be a really worrying time for dad/partner, too, as the options presented all carry risk, some more than others, and are just another thing to have to get your head around! I entered my labour hoping, understandably, for a simple birth, so when I was faced with more interventions than you could throw a stick at, I freaked out. And once the ordeal was over, I was left with the mental and emotional discomfort, as well as the physical. Another mother told me that she'd never anticipated that she would want more pain relief as a result of needing an assisted birth, and that she felt in some way that she'd failed because she needed, in her words 'bloody everything on offer!'

Some of the most common interventions or assisted birth procedures are:

Induction

According to NHS Maternity Statistics, more than one in four women need an induction procedure to help get labour kick-started for one reason or another.

Labour can be induced using a pessary, which is a small almond-shaped tablet that a medical professional inserts into your vagina to slowly release a substance called prostaglandin (naturally found in the womb lining) that should soften the cervix and encourage contractions. In some cases, when things need to be moved on more quickly, waters can be artificially broken by the midwife using an amnio hook (a bit like a crochet hook) to painlessly rupture the membrane/sack, or an artificial hormone called syntocinon can be given through a drip in the arm to get contractions started or going again. In some cases labour may have already started but slowed down or stopped altogether and so needs a bit of a boost – like jump-starting a car engine.

During induced labour, often the contractions come on quite quickly, with the result that because there hasn't been time to let either them or your levels of the natural pain-killer hormone beta-endorphin gradually build up, they can feel stronger and more painful than contractions that start naturally, and there may be shorter intervals for recovery in between. This may lead to you needing strong pain relief, such as an epidural.

Forceps and ventouse

In the UK, 13 per cent of babies are born by forceps or ventouse – two different instruments that can help deliver a baby.

Forceps are a surgical instrument that comes in two halves and looks like large salad tongs. Each half is carefully put round the baby's head while it is in the birth canal, and the two handles fit together. The doctor pulls at the same time as you push with a contraction (if you can), to assist in getting the baby out.

A ventouse is a silicone cap attached to a suction pump. The cap is fitted on the baby's head while it is in the birth canal and is kept in place using suction. The ventouse is then pulled, as for the forceps delivery, to help the baby be born.

According to the NHS, using forceps is more likely to be successful than a ventouse. However, ventouse delivery is less invasive, takes up less space in the vaginal canal, and as such doesn't always require you to have an episiotomy – so is sometimes the first option. Forceps are often used if a ventouse hasn't worked, and its use brings an increased risk of complications for the woman in labour such as potential tears to the perineum (the area between the vagina and the bottom).

Episiotomy

An episiotomy is a deliberate surgical cut to the vagina, often made by the doctor just before the baby is born. It's aim is to reduce the risk of sustaining a vaginal tear (which can be harder to heal from), widen the opening (perhaps for forceps or ventouse delivery), and allow the baby to be born more quickly. This is repaired using stitches under local anaesthetic following the birth.

Caesarean (C-section)

A Caesarean is an operation that allows your baby to be born without going through the birth canal. Instead, they're born through a cut in your abdomen.

A Caesarean birth involves major abdominal surgery, although this can usually be done with a type of anaesthetic, such as an epidural, that allows you to remain awake if you want.

There are two types of Caesarean section (C-section) – planned (elective) and unplanned (emergency). A planned C-section is scheduled to take place before labour starts and it may be planned for medical reasons, such as the position of the baby, or solely due to the mother's request. In chapter 9 I talk more about elective C-sections , why you might want to consider it, and what the current NICE guidelines say. It is becoming increasingly common for women who have experienced a traumatic vaginal birth to opt for a planned C-section the next time round – according to the NCT elective C-sections are up year on year and now account for 13 per cent of births in the UK.

More than one in six of us need an emergency C-section. These take place quickly because an unexpected problem has arisen and the baby needs to be born as soon as possible. This decision is usually made when you are already in labour and it can be very fraught and traumatic for all involved.

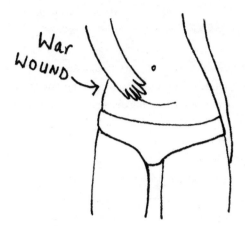

Now, you may have experienced one or more of these procedures, or you may have been spared the added inconvenience that an assisted birth, or birth intervention, creates... Regardless, most women come out the other side of giving birth with a few war wounds to write home about.

> *'With my first labour*
> *I remember physically feeling like I had*
> *been hit by a bus, two-and-a-half hours of pushing*
> *followed by an episiotomy and ventouse delivery*
> *left me fairly bruised and battered, but I also felt*
> *like I could take on the world for those first 24 hours.*
> *Even now, I feel like my two labours are my*
> *greatest achievement.'*
>
> **Ana – mum of two**

Breaking point

IF PERHAPS you're yet to give birth, or you're supporting someone who's about to and want to give some helpful advice, remember that YOU are in charge of your baby and body. Ask questions as much as you want and need in order to help you feel as clued up, and as in control of what's to come, as you're able to.

FOCUS ON the end goal. In those moments of 'OMG I can't do this', tell yourself that you CAN, and visualise the very end moment, when you get to meet your baby, as the motivation to keep going.

MAKE A FUSS! If you're feeling unsure or scared in any way, make sure you tell someone and *ask for extra help*, reassurance, and if you want it, as much pain relief as you darn well choose.

NO MATTER how challenging it can feel, remember that labour WILL come to an end before long. Do whatever you need and want to do and *never ever* feel as though you're being a nuisance or a wuss.

'The baby and I were put in a side room and pretty much left there on our own. I felt completely out of it; a strong part of me just wanted to fall asleep in exhaustion as I was wiped out but the other part was looking at the baby in the cot next to me and starting to panic a bit about what I was supposed to be doing.'

Suki – mum to IVF baby Eddie

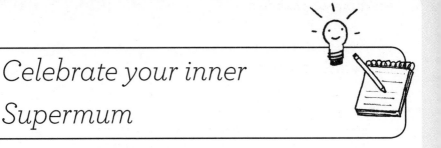

Celebrate your inner Supermum

This exercise is intended to help you embrace the positive aspects of your birth and in the process let any negative or uncomfortable feelings you might be experiencing take a momentary back seat. Our mind is super powerful and we can help ease off any physical discomfort by kicking our imagination and senses into action. Don't believe me? Why not have a go?

Find a time when it's most likely that there'll be a moment of calm and you can just 'be'. It might be mid breast/bottle feed, on the loo, perhaps in the middle of a bath or shower, and allow this time (even if just a few sacred minutes) to be just YOU.

During these precious few minutes, you are going to give your body and mind permission to leave any pains, niggles or twinges behind, safe in the knowledge that anything you might be feeling physically as a result of giving birth is also due to your body achieving the most amazing thing – producing a baby.

As you reflect on this single thought, allow yourself to feel proud of yourself. Wow, you actually did it! How incredible are you?! Thank your body for doing an amazing job.

Now, take a lovely big, deep breath, close your eyes, and cast your mind back to the moments just after your baby arrived. Focus on anything positive from that experience... Perhaps you remember the first time you clapped eyes on your baby, maybe you can recall the first sniff of that lovely unique baby smell, recalling your baby's first cry, signalling that all was well, how about holding baby's tiny hand for the first time, or perhaps you felt instant relief that he/she was now here and any pain was over...

Take notice of all those feelings, anything you felt, saw, or heard... Recall all the good things, no matter how tiny and insignificant they might seem, and allow those positive experiences to fill your mind and body.

Allow the feel-good remembered feelings to flood through your body like a warm wave passing from head to toe, and as you allow those memories to engulf you, enjoy how they make you feel.

With these lovely thoughts and feelings passing through your body, allow yourself to smile at the memories, and make every feeling and thought better, brighter and sharper. For example, if you feel warm and fuzzy when remembering your baby gazing up at you as you do skin-on-skin bonding for the first time, make this feeling even warmer, more glowing and perhaps even give it a warm colour such as yellow like that of the summer sun.

Let your imagination go wild and make everything good about your birth – and there will be *something* even if you have to dig deep – as wonderful as you possibly can.

In the final few moments of letting yourself get lost in this wonderful memory, take another long, slow, deep breath and as you exhale, open your eyes and give yourself a jolly good 'well done me'.

This is a nice quick little activity for those 'ouch' recovery days, when you perhaps need to give yourself a bit of a boost.

Other yuck stuff

Whether you've had birth invention or delivered your baby without needing one, with perhaps the exception of a C-section, our private parts are likely to feel a little battered and bruised – after all, don't they say it's the equivalent of pooing a melon?! Ouch.

Other yukky and unsettling stuff also happens to us ladies in the aftermath, and the physical task of childbirth and what it leaves behind can have a huge impact mentally, causing feelings of anxiety, worry and low mood. This is completely normal – after all, if you weren't just the teensiest bit worried or nervous about the state of your tender fanny, or anxious about the engorged leaky boobs you've suddenly developed, it'd be a bit odd right? I remember one new mum pal messaging our group in the middle of the night announcing she was actually quite freaked out about her massive 'burger nipples' and asking 'would they ever shrink down again?!'

The physical changes my body was going through in the run-up to giving birth were certainly more than a little worrying and anxiety inducing. My boobs in particular scared the bejeezus out of me... I used to pride myself on having a pretty good pair of 34Ds but, fast forward a couple of decades and having suddenly developed nipples the size of dinner plates, a rather disturbing shade of 'bruise' purple, and leaking yellow honey-like liquid (the magic colostrum) and then, later, spurting milk all over the shop, I was more than a little irked.

Then there's the post-birth 'puff' as I call it. The best way I can tastefully describe my under-carriage after all the pulling, pushing and shoving it had endured, is that it felt like a miniature inflatable lilo had been attached in between my legs. The horror at putting my hand 'down below' to assess the damage and feel my stitches was more than a little distressing – I genuinely worried if I would ever have nookie again (not that I wanted it mind!). It's true when they say one's dignity is left firmly at the door when you give birth, and, for me, that really is true – I'd gone from going bright red in embarrassment during a smear test to not giving a flying toss who looked 'down there', so desperate was I to be reassured that it was OK and going to be normal again. It was, and it is, thankfully.

Having to have stitches was something I feared big time, but it turns out it was one of the easiest and relatively painless parts of the whole shebang – a great reminder of how anticipation can often be so much worse than the actual event. In fact, so many mums say that the stuff they really feared before giving birth didn't actually come to fruition. One lady told me how she was fearful, to the point of having a panic attack, about delivering her placenta as she was squeamish about it, yet when it actually came to it yes she felt the milder contractions but she a) was too distracted by her new baby, and b) she never even saw it, so quickly was it whipped away by a midwife. Of course this isn't always the case, as we've already discussed, but the point is that some things turn out to be nowhere near as awful as we imagine them to be.

> *'I found it really surreal actually meeting the baby that had been a "bump" for the last nine months. It was not until I met him that it became real for me. Physically I felt knackered and was quite scared to move as I didn't know what state my body was in.'*
>
> **Hannah – mum to George, aged 11 months**

Something else that really bothered me and was a major anxiety trigger was all the post-birth 'stuff' that us women lose after childbirth – I'm talking about the post-birth bleed they call lochia. I remember my NCT teacher warning us expectant parents not to buy a cream sofa or even THINK about sitting on a lightly coloured chair after giving birth! This put the fear into me big time, and ramped my anxiety up more than a little bit at the thought of potential leaks through my massive maternity pads (what an unsexy bit of kit they are eh!), and ruining other people's upholstery. In reality it really wasn't half as bad as I'd been led to believe, although many people do experience heavy bleeding and passing of clots for days and even weeks after birth. If you've had a C-section, this is less likely since the docs manually remove the placenta and as much 'debris' as possible while you are on the operating table, whereas if you have a vaginal birth it all has to come out of its own accord. Either way, the bleeding does eventually end, and if you are well prepared it isn't something to be too freaked out by.

The water retention and bloating meant I honestly looked like a Michelin Man. I puffed up about four dress sizes the minute I had Enzo – I thought you were supposed to LOSE weight the minute you pop a weighty baby and placenta out, not gain it?! Add to that the constipating iron tablets, getting the hang of breastfeeding (more on this later), and the general bruised and delicate feeling, it's safe to say I definitely knew I'd just gone through a major life moment, and hadn't just sneezed a baby out Hollywood-style.

But you know what, for all of the physical wear and tear childbirth undoubtedly takes on our bodies, it's really is a testament to Mother Nature how it repairs and eventually heals itself – in a lot of cases, until it's like new. Despite this, there's no doubt that the early days and weeks of anxiety, worry and stress that I felt, and I know countless others also endure, weren't helped by all the physical stuff happening to my body, too.

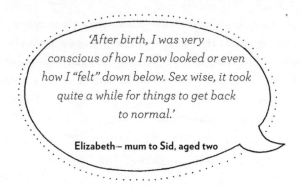

'After birth, I was very conscious of how I now looked or even how I "felt" down below. Sex wise, it took quite a while for things to get back to normal.'

Elizabeth – mum to Sid, aged two

Holy crap!!

There is no other topic that I talk about on social media that gets quite as much traction and 'likes' as Pooing in Peace.

If you're the partner, friend or relative of someone with a little one then let me tell you now, if there is one charitable thing you can do for a mum of a newborn, then that is to babysit while they pop off for a number two. There is no greater joy than being able to use the loo in peace, and crucially, by yourself. I know, it sounds absurd until it happens to you, but the moment there's a baby in the mix, you can kiss goodbye to the privacy of being able to go to the toilet for as long you like/need – and if you've been put on a course of those dreaded constipating iron tablets then may the force be with you!

A poignant moment was when I had to take my crying 10-day-old son into the loo with me, strap him into a sling on my chest to soothe him and then artfully contort myself in order to 'do my business' without gassing the poor mite. A low point for us both (sorry son). I howled with laughter swapping poo stories with a work pal who empathetically shared that she's fed up with getting her knees bashed on a daily basis by the occupied baby walker following her as she squats on the loo!

'Going for your "first poo" is a surreal experience. Never have I had so many people genuinely pleased and proud of me for having a s**t.'

Ola – mum of baby girl

And then there's even being able to GO to the loo in the first place – poo anxiety. Is there a more terrifying moment than going for your first poo after giving birth? I think not. Some 24 hours post-partum I waddled along the hospital corridor, open-backed gown flapping exposing my massive Primark knickers, one hand clutching a brick-sized sanitary pad, the other an NHS cardboard poo container as it was deemed easier to sit on and aim into than the actual lavatory. Not since I was a potty training three-year-old have so many people of authority (the midwives on this occasion, not my mother) been so obsessed with whether I've done a poo or not! 'We just need to check that's it's all working m'love' they said...

Hanging on to the sink and hovering over the container, one eye closed, wincing in expectation at what might come – this was a new form of anxiety to add to my already quite wide range. What if I can't poo? Will they keep me in another night? Will my stiches hold...? My fears were very real, but in reality even though it wasn't my finest, most enjoyable of loo moments, it certainly wasn't half as bad as I'd been fearing. The elation at being able to produce what the midwives wanted me to, and still being intact at the end of my efforts, was worthy of a little whoop and high five to myself in the bathroom mirror.

I know it's not ladylike but I don't care what anyone says, toilet anxiety is a thing. A big thing and one that becomes a whole new ball game once you're a parent. What with keeping the wretched pelvic floor muscles intact, timing your motorway service-station stops to accommodate said pelvic-floor accidents, and finding more than a 60-second window out of your day in which to have a poo between feeds without giving yourself piles or an anal fissure by rushing it (and I've done both), going to the loo is a big deal.

How to... have a successful post-birth poo and pee

Getting your bodily functions back on track after birth is a stressful time: try these handy hints to make it that little bit easier.

IF YOU'RE on iron tablets, make sure you drink lots and lots of water to help moisten any excrement waiting to come out. Iron-tablet poos are the *worst* so help yourself by keeping hydrated.

EAT lots of poo-inducing foods that are high in fibre, such as dried fruits (good old prunes are the best), wholemeal bread, pulses, nuts and bran-based cereals.

DON'T RUSH IT! Rushing a poo is only going to cause more damage in the long run... Breathe your poo out rhythmically, and get someone to watch the baby and any other children while you're in the bathroom so you can take your time.

DON'T BE ALARMED if blood clots come out as you do a poo. Straining, even gently, is likely to cause your lochia to increase in the early days. This is a good opportunity to assess the size and colour of those clots, and seek help if they are larger than they should be or are worrying in appearance (your midwife or doctor can tell you what is and isn't OK).

IF YOU NEED to... poo in the bath! The warm water can help the act feel a little easier, less painful, and the water also helps in diluting the stingy acidity of an accompanying wee.

IF YOU ARE concerned that you may have burst your stitches while on the loo or that everything is more painful than it should be, seek help as soon as you can. Too many people ignore excessive pain and it can be a sign of infection that needs treating urgently.

YOU CAN also pour a cup of warm water over your front bits as you wee to help with the stinging, although be aware that getting all the water in the loo is quite tricky and it's likely some will go on the floor.

PELVIC FLOOR! We all get nagged to do them, we all forget to do them, but pelvic floor exercises really do help in strengthening the muscles down below post birth. Pull up your pelvic floor (like you are holding in a wee mid flow) and hold and pulse for three seconds, relax, and then repeat 10 times. Do this several times a day – I try to do it every time I brush my teeth or boil the kettle so I vaguely remember.

IT'S LIKELY that your pelvic floor will be fairly weak for a while, even if you do your exercises religiously, so you may feel more secure if you wear pads in order to avoid any embarrassing accidents. And perhaps give trampolining a miss for a few months...

Will I ever be the same again?

The connection between physical and mental health is such a biggy that I'll also be touching on other aspects of it in later chapters. The immediate changes are plentiful and can be more than a little overwhelming at times – particularly in those first sleep-deprived days, weeks and months, it can feel huge. The one thing you should take great comfort in is that ultimately, you will always be 'you', but perhaps just a different version of yourself – a *new* you: a parent. And all that this new role throws at you will challenge and make you a stronger, more rounded person as a result. Yes, it can be tough, with lots of little hurdles to tackle along the way as we all adapt to this new way of life, but in between you will get smiles and adoring gazes from your little one – and even in those crap moments, it genuinely makes everything feel 10 times better.

So, my friend, read on for plenty more about the other side of birth, including feeling too anxious to eat, living with a little Sleep Thief, and the million-dollar question a lot of new parents eventually find themselves pondering: 'when to have sex again?!'

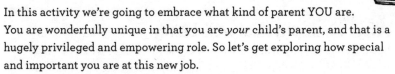

Who do you think you are?

In this activity we're going to embrace what kind of parent YOU are. You are wonderfully unique in that you are *your* child's parent, and that is a hugely privileged and empowering role. So let's get exploring how special and important you are at this new job.

First up I want you to list your values (what's important to you) as a parent, for example some of my values are:

Love
Security
Patience
Communication
Boundaries
Trust
Loyalty
Hard work
Forgiveness
Honesty
Health
Freedom
Companionship
Family and friends
Independence
You can list as many of these values as you like.

Once you've done this, you can go one step further and add to each one what belief you hold that reinforces this value, for example mine is:

Value: love = belief: 'I have a loving, supportive family and together we will give Vincenzo all the love in the world he needs to help him feel safe.'

By working through your values and beliefs as a parent you can figure out what's important to you – and that really is all that matters. If you are confident and assured about what kind of good parent you are, everyone wins.

Dr Reetta says...

After birth physical well-being After the birth you are
healing from the physical process and at the same time dealing with all
the changes to your daily life since your baby arrived. As Anna experienced, the physical challenges and changes during and following birth
can be major, and can include being exhausted due to not sleeping or
eating well, and not exercising. You have a baby who cannot tell you
what they need. There is a lot going on.

Relaxation is one of the best ways to make yourself feel better,
especially if you are in physical pain post-birth, because the more tense
you are, the worse the pain will feel. Learning how to relax isn't easy for
many of us – you may be someone who has never learned to truly let go!
Or you may be good at it, but now that your baby is here, you might
need to re-think how to do it. Let's take a look at two types of relaxation:
with and without your baby. Remember, relaxation is a skill, an attitude
and a habit, so expect it to take time, practice and patience. Learning
relaxation skills will give you more energy, and help you feel less
anxious and tense. In addition, being together closely or skin to skin
with your baby produces oxytocin, the 'love hormone', which helps with
bonding and relaxation too.

Top tips for looking after your physical well-being

1. Build moments of relaxation into your daily routine *with* your
baby. Do this when your baby is content. Lie down on your bed or
on the sofa with your baby. Just be there, breathe deeply, look at
your baby, study their features, listen to their breathing, smell
their smell, stroke their skin, cuddle them. Babies love faces and
physical contact. You may find your baby staring at your face and
enjoying imitating your facial expressions. By the time your baby

is two months old, they will start smiling, which will make these moments of relaxation even more rewarding.

2. Build moments of relaxation into your daily routine *without* your baby. You may think you are relaxing when you are watching TV or on social media, but this is not *true* relaxation (however much these activities can be enjoyable). True relaxation will bring on the relaxation response (a feeling of calm in your body and mind), which is the opposite of the stress response (when your mind and body are in fight-or-flight mode). Schedule a time in your day to do some active relaxation, such as deep breathing or muscle relaxation, whereby you mentally engage in the relaxation process.

3. Do some problem solving by setting small goals around diet/ nutrition, sleep/rest and physical exercise. These will be individual for everyone, depending on your circumstances pre-baby and now. Thinking about these three areas may be the last thing in your mind, but I would encourage you to dedicate *some* thought to this. One positive change in one area is likely to lead to other positive changes in other areas. For example, physical exercise, such as going for a walk with your baby, is not only going to reduce tension and boost your mood, but can also help you to clear your mind and gain more balanced perspective on your thoughts.

Quick relaxation exercise

Reduce any physical tension by scanning your body and then 'squeezing and releasing' those body parts. You can do this lying down or sitting. Bring your attention to each part of your body one at a time, noticing the physical sensations, starting from your toes and working towards the top of your head. When you notice tension, squeeze and then release those muscles. If you need a bit more guidance, try relaxation exercises on YouTube or mindfulness apps. *Mind the Bump* is a good app specifically for new and expecting parents, while *Headspace* is a good generic app – both full of relaxation, breathing and mindfulness exercises.

4
GROUNDHOG DAY

The 'tick tock, slave to the clock' feeling

Parenting is a constant battle between going to bed to catch up on some sleep, or staying awake to finally get some alone time.

Baby steps...

NOTHING CAN prepare you for the shock of bringing your baby home and having to suddenly be a parent. Rest assured that everyone feels some level of panic and it DOES get easier.

ONE MOMENT at a time, one day at a time. Don't feel you have to be perfect – nobody is – particularly when it comes to parenting. Go with the flow and trust your instincts.

DON'T GO IT ALONE. Whether it's a partner, family member, friend or an online forum such as Netmums or Mumsnet, reach out, and keep talking and sharing how you're feeling as you adjust – it really helps!

The first day of the rest of your life

I think it's pretty fair to say that the first day of becoming a parent is one of THE most daunting days you will ever experience. There are few other life events that can top the overwhelming feeling of sudden responsibility that being a mum or dad brings – it is completely and utterly consuming.

After three nights of no sleep at the hospital I'd given birth in I was so desperate for some peace and quiet that I begged my husband to take us home. (I could handle the other crying babies and recovering mothers, but the nurses' station buzzer that went off like the *Family Fortunes* TV show 'uh oh' buzzer nearly sent me over the edge!)

I'm not alone: most mothers I speak to say that they couldn't wait to escape the noisy maternity wards and seek solace in the comfort of their own home. Unless you're one of the lucky ones who get a plush side room, the racket of the general hustle and bustle in a post-labour ward is akin to a street party at times!

The momentary excitement of getting out of the hospital and back to a comfy couch, decent cup of tea and unlimited Netflix was extremely short-lived. Once the medical team deemed us well enough to leave, the sudden reality dawned on me... oh shit, I'm going to be leaving the on-tap pain-relief drugs and midwifery advice, and going it alone. The level of anxiety I felt at being allowed to leave, and also due to the realisation that this new little person was now my sole responsibility, was something I'd never felt before – and for a GAD and panic-attack sufferer, that's saying something!

Trussing up our beautiful little son in his obligatory going-home outfit, our stress levels were certainly tested as it took my other half and I a good 10 minutes to work out how the hell to fix him into the new car-seat-carrier-thing. We'd had a demonstration in John Lewis where the salesman had used some weird-looking doll, but it turns out it's a whole thing using an *actual* baby. They are just so tiny and have alarmingly wobbly heads!

Walking out of the reassuring sanctity of the maternity ward, I wanted to run straight back in again. I didn't feel ready... What if I couldn't cope? What if the baby got ill? What if I didn't recover quickly enough? What if I was just crap at being a mum? The anxiety festered and bubbled, like trapped wind after a curry, and we felt like complete novices strapping our little chap into the back seat of the car. But then we all are – the first time round we're all complete and utter novices. I can only imagine the anxiety Prince William must have felt buckling little Prince George in to his 4x4 *in front of the world's media*. And as for Kate, how she managed to get in the car in such a ladylike fashion, and not have to haul herself into the seat arse first holding on to the door handle, beats me.

Arriving home, assuming you haven't had a home birth and are therefore already cocooned in your own manor, is a surreal experience. Ask any new parent how they felt walking through their front door with a new person in tow, and they'll no doubt tell you how very strange it is. Like someone has given you a very unpredictable bike, taken the stabilisers off and ordered you to immediately give the Tour de France a crack. If you're anything like us, my hubby carried our new baby into our house (I tottered in after them gingerly, looking pathetic) and then plonked him on the lounge floor all snug and sleepy in his car seat. We looked at each other, somewhat stunned, and said 'now what?!' We just stared at him, at each other – too nervous to even leave him for a moment to pop to the loo.

The first day of the rest of our lives had officially started, we were now parents and we didn't have the foggiest idea what to do. It was like someone had lobbed a slowly, silently ticking hand grenade into our living room, stuck their fingers in their ears and scarpered sharpish, leaving us to deal with the inevitable explosion that would ultimately shatter the peace of the moment.

We were wide-eyed newbies on the first day of school, and I for one was not coping too well with the massive life change. The physical fatigue and the emotional and mental impact of going from 'Anna' to 'mummy' was terrifying, and this fear more than hindered my first few weeks and months of motherhood.

Lots of new parents speak of those nerve-wracking first few days and weeks. One couple told me that they thought they'd be more than prepared as they had a dog and were used to its demands and the 'tie' it created. They genuinely laughed at their own naïvety as they spoke of the reality of a baby joining the family causing far more upheaval and mess than taking the pooch for a walk twice a day.

Other parents speak of the sheer shock they feel, and overwhelming responsibility of suddenly becoming a parent overnight. There really is nothing that can prepare you for it. However, DO remember that no matter how overwhelmed you may feel, you are most certainly not alone.

Breaking Point   S.O.S

YOU'VE JUST BECOME a parent and you're freaking out about the new responsibility placed on you. Make use of your midwives and health visitors and be brave and tell them how you're feeling – it's natural to feel shocked the moment you become mum or dad.

DON'T FEEL you have to blag it – if you don't know what to do with your new baby then don't busk it, it's perfectly normal to not have a clue. Ask for help and advice from family members, friends, and health professionals – how to change a nappy, bath baby, feed etc.

TAKE ONE DAY at a time. Try not to run before you can walk. Babies are scary... they are unpredictable and you haven't worked how he or she 'works' yet. It takes time to get used to, and even to like, your new baby.

*'All I wanted to do was
sleep but obviously I just couldn't. I felt
so resentful to my husband and these babies.
I can't say I had an actual bond and that made
me feel like the worst person on earth. After all,
having children was all I ever wanted.'*

Katie – mum of triplets

Feeling the heat

In the first few days and weeks of being a parent, the level of visitors and 'pop-ins' is relentless. The best advice I was given in the last stages of pregnancy was to put a 'come back in a week – just leave food on the doorstep' sign on the front door and batten down the hatches as your little family adjusts. It's a nice idea in principle, in fact it's a glorious fantasy, but the reality is you will probably struggle to keep the well-wishers and Interflora deliveries at bay from the minute you arrive back home.

Not for one moment am I being ungrateful for the incredible kindness and generosity that was bestowed on us in celebration of our new arrival, but if I could turn back the clock, I would have appreciated it all so much more a few months further down the line when my head wasn't such a frazzled mess.

Of course, this is impossible – Great Auntie Janice and co aren't going to be fobbed off for a moment longer than possible, so most of us just have to grin and bear it, put our exhaustion and discomfort to one side (again), and allow the world and his wife to traipse into our living rooms to coo and cluck over the sleeping little bundle as we plaster on our public face. I get it, it's hugely exciting when a new baby arrives for everyone, I've been (and still am) that annoying friend/relative that rocks up merely hours after someone has given birth to offer my congratulations and the obligatory babygro/nipple cream gift basket.

The adjustment time for any new parent should not be underestimated and is hugely personal for each fledgling family, and most parents feel the heat of juggling the massive life change. I have spoken to mothers of adopted children, parents of IVF-conceived babies, and mums and dads of surrogates and multiples, and no matter 'how' we all become parents, everyone is unanimous in stressing how important those initial weeks of bonding and learning are.

If you're anything like me, I was so affected by the birth and change that had just happened that the last thing I wanted to do was entertain... is there a more exposing situation? Sitting in my PJs, ghost white with shock and probably anaemia, foggy with sleep deprivation and highly anxious about anything and everything, the last thing I felt like doing was chatting over a cuppa. I was so worried about being judged, about looking like I wasn't coping, and coming across as a total failure. I'd been so out of it after the birth that I missed the midwife's lesson on nappy changing, so I couldn't even do that properly at first.

Several mum friends also recall those first few weeks of getting to grips with their new baby, and coping with the intense anxiety that comes with trying to gauge what the heck to do and when, the tricky task of feeding smack bang in the middle of yet another well-wisher's visit, and having to be OK with your precious new bundle being passed around like a rugby ball.

'Watching my week-old baby
being picked up by relative after relative, all
I wanted to do was scream "give her back to me!"
I had such an overwhelming urge and need to hold
her myself it was almost too much to bear to have
others fussing over her.'

Alessandra – mum to Liliana, aged four months

Breaking Point

S.O.S

GIVE YOURSELF a break each day – it's super important for keeping anxiety at bay. Either with or without your baby, if you can find a willing friend or partner to babysit them and any other children you have, take yourself for a walk outdoors, breathe in the air (hopefully fresh), and get those endorphins going – a natural mood booster and anxiety reducer.

IF YOU CAN, get a mum or friend to watch your baby and any other kids for an hour or so or, even better, why not take yourself to the local swimming pool for a swim and sauna, or perhaps the gym for a relaxation class – or even just to a cafe to get a change of scene, and sit and have an uninterrupted cup of tea.

IF YOU HAVE OLDER CHILDREN, you will probably be feeling guilty about neglecting them, so it can be extremely reassuring for both them and you if you can get someone else to look after the baby for a while so you can spend some quality time with the other little people in your life. It is often best to just do something simple that you used to enjoy together before everything was turned upside down by the arrival of the youngest member of the family, such as going to the playground, playing a game, or making some cakes.

Anxiety overload

Anxiety is something a lot of parents identify with, and with all the dos and don'ts of having a child, it's no wonder so many of us are feeling the heat – there's just so much to learn and/or remember. When we feel anxious, we're more often than not on high alert, with bucket-loads of adrenalin coursing round our bodies. This can result in us being totally wired to ensure that nothing happens to the baby, in full-on protective mode, or sometimes in completely the opposite 'actually I hate this, just get me out of here' mode.

Chances are you'll have experienced some form of anxiety in your life at some point – work deadlines, speaking in public, flying on an aeroplane... It's a very normal reaction to a stressful or concerning situation, and also a very useful and necessary built-in tool we each have. Back in caveman days anxiety took on the form often referred to now as fight, flight or freeze mode – a response within our brains that was triggered when it perceived threat was imminent. Either you ran away from the threat, you fought it head on, or you froze in fright, a little bit like a deer in headlights, as the fear and shock caused momentary paralysis.

Anxiety is like an inner alarm or panic button to alert us to a potentially threatening situation. It can serve us well by, for example, stopping us walking out in front of a passing car, or by giving us a little adrenalin boost to deliver a presentation well. But sometimes anxiety can be more of a hindrance than a help. You may well have never had any issues before you became a parent but, suddenly faced with the life changes that having a baby – even if it's not your first – brings, you may feel niggles of anxiety, and perhaps even experience panic attacks, which is what can happen when anxiety ramps up to a point at which it needs to escape, and that can be more than a little scary. Anxiety and panic attacks can also come with some rather annoying, upsetting and very real-feeling physical symptoms.

Anxiety has always presented itself for me as a horribly debilitating fizz of energy that takes over my whole body and centres in my chest area. I feel dizzy, short of breath and hot all over. I also often need the loo – a rather embarrassing symptom as the body temporarily shuts down the digestive system in order to send adrenalin to the rest of the body quickly to deal with the threat. In the moment, it's horrible, yet, although it's often misguided, I know that the anxiety is either trying to alert me to protect myself or those around me, and to be highly vigilant to the point of exhaustion (fight mode), or it makes me want to run away from everyone and everything as fast as my legs will carry me (flight mode). Sometimes I just clamp up and I have no clue what to do (freeze mode). I just can't cope. The anxiety just takes over. And I have no idea which way it will swing until I'm in the moment.

My anxiety and mental health was so bad in those early first days. I also wasn't eating, as I couldn't physically swallow food (when I'm anxious I feel like my throat is closing up – nasty). In a constant state of low-level panic my body was in shock and went into shut-down mode. I'd been here before though – so I pretty quickly realised I needed medical help. My health visitor was particularly on it thankfully, and fortunately I'm good at being open and honest about my mental health and asking for help, as I had been throughout my pregnancy. But there was still a bit of me that worried I would be labelled a failure... I'm only human after all. So many of us are scared of being open about our feelings – it can feel so hard to admit we're not coping, or feeling far from overjoyed with our new baby. But having been there I can't emphasise enough how the more you let others in and help you, the easier it becomes.

My husband had recognised I was displaying symptoms of my previous anxiety disorder – the lack of appetite, I was scared to be left alone, unable to make a decision on anything – and he suggested I talk to the post-natal team when they next came over. So, after a long chat over a cuppa at home with my health visitor about how I was feeling, during which she asked if I was having any negative thoughts about myself or the baby (I was), we agreed that it would be a good idea for me to see my doctor for some further support. After making an appointment with my GP, I explained how I was feeling, that I wasn't enjoying motherhood particularly and was extremely anxious about everything. I have been on anti-depressants and anxiety medication in the past and I knew that I needed some of the same assistance again. The doctor was empathetic, thankfully, and I felt so grateful that someone had the means and advice to help me feel better. After a discussion with him during which he asked if I'd like to carry on with breastfeeding (I did), I initially agreed to go on a breastfeeding-compatible anti-depressant, Sertraline.

Anti-anxiety and depression medication (called selective serotonin reuptake inhibitors – SSRIs) work for some but don't for others – it's a very personal experience and choice. I'm a big fan of medication when appropriate as it has really helped me. That said, I firmly believe it should always be used in conjunction with some form of talking therapy to help work through the issues and feelings, so reliance on the pills is kept to a minimum. In addition to the medication I was taking to help balance out my brain chemicals, I also had a few phone counselling sessions with my psychiatrist, and I also went to see a local psychologist who specialised in post-natal mental health – both these approaches together were essential and invaluable in supporting my fragile state of mind.

Sadly, though, the medication chosen might have been compatible with my breast milk but it certainly wasn't compatible with me! The advice is always to allow a period of a few weeks for medication to take effect, but after just four days on this particular anti-depressant I felt more zombified and out of it than ever before. I was also starting to feel really guilty about resenting my baby for needing to feed from me. I just needed to feel well again.

Something had to change – and quick. After another consultation with my doctor, we agreed that a change in my medication was necessary, to a commonly used drug called Escitalopram. However, due to its ingredients, this would mean I would have to stop breastfeeding my son immediately – a very tough and emotional decision, and one laced with guilt, but ultimately I had to make the right call for my son AND me. After all, don't they say 'happy mum, happy baby'? For me, it was the right decision and one I'm really pleased I made sooner rather than later in order to take the pressure off (therefore reducing the anxiety), and allowing me to start nurturing my relationship with my boy. I'll be delving more into the breastfeeding and medication topics in the next chapter.

Breaking Point
$\boxed{\text{S.O.S}}$

IF, LIKE MANY PEOPLE, you're unsure about taking medication for mental health-related illnesses, ask yourself, 'what is it I'm worried about?' Often it's the stigma of being on pills, and some people also feel wary about any side effects and reliance. Remember though, medication is there to HELP if and when you might need it.

ALWAYS TALK TO a medical professional such as your GP or a psychiatrist to discuss if this is a route worth looking into – and, crucially, for how long you might need to take it. Coming off any medication should always be monitored by your doctor and done gradually.

YOU SHOULD always consider a talking therapy alongside any medication support to help work through any underlying issues. A GP can help with referrals. There is no shame, only strength, in asking for help when things get tough.

'Those first two weeks were crap to be honest. I felt cheated that I wasn't enjoying it all as much as I thought I should. I worried about the baby's health and my self-esteem just took a nose dive. My emotions were all over the place.'

Sally – mum to James, aged 12 months

The insider's guide to panic attacks

We looked at post-natal anxiety in chapter 2, but it's helpful to know that there are so many scenarios that can make us feel anxious and trigger anxiety attacks, without it developing into an actual mental health condition. Sleepless nights, a baby's persistent crying, not being able to settle baby, juggling work-life-family, fitting in with peers, feeling nervous in social settings, coping with a poorly baby, rowing with your other half, feeling guilty about neglecting other children... you name it, so many scenarios can cause moments of 'eek' where you might need a helping hand at getting a handle on it.

Experiencing a panic attack can feel truly horrible. Some people liken it to how a heart attack might feel, and in the heat of the moment many sufferers (including me), say it feels like you're going to die. Rest assured – you won't.

How to... recognise if you're having a panic attack

YOU MIGHT feel some of the following symptoms: a tight or 'stabby' chest, heart pumping faster, the sensation that it's hard to breathe, you might get dizzy, feel red in the face or go white as a sheet, feel faint, sweaty, you might need the loo (number one AND two), have a dry mouth, loss of appetite, feel sick, nauseous, hot, cold...

IF YOU FEEL any of these symptoms, you most probably are experiencing a pesky panic attack, so make sure you find yourself a safe space in which to sit down, then take some nice deep breaths – in through the nose and out through the mouth. If you can, tell someone how you're feeling so they can sit with you while it passes.

IT'S IMPORTANT to rule out anything more serious than a panic attack so do call a medical professional if you're in any way concerned and want a professional opinion – better to be safe than sorry.

OK, now we've looked at how it can feel to experience anxiety or a panic attack, let's have a go at trying to get one under control. The main tip is not to fight or resist it. Think of any such attack like a naughty child... the more you tell it 'no', the harder it tries to succeed. The moment you give in, lose interest in trying to get it under control and just allow it to run out of steam, is the moment it loses its interest, and its hold over you or the situation.

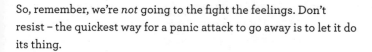

Conquering a panic attack

So, remember, we're *not* going to the fight the feelings. Don't resist – the quickest way for a panic attack to go away is to let it do its thing.

If and when possible, get yourself to a safe place, where you can just 'be' for a few moments in private, eg the bathroom, loo, quiet corner, the car in the supermarket car park – making sure your baby and any other children are confined in a safe place. Now challenge your panic attack to 'come on, do your worst'.

Allow any feelings to peak (they won't stay there long, I promise) and then allow them to wash over you like a cool, calming wave, and notice how they dissolve out and away from your body.

Stay in the present. Notice where you are, your surroundings, focus on the hardness of the surface you're sitting on, what you can hear – eg other people talking, passing traffic, birds tweeting – and remind yourself how safe you are.

Notice what's really happening to you, not what you think might happen.

Check on your breathing, too. First, sit down if you can, or stand up nice and upright but in a physically relaxed way – shoulders down, shake your hands out to release any tension and roll your head gently from side to side to ease out any tension there.

Close your eyes and focus solely on your breathing – your in and out breath. How does it feel and sound? We want to make that breathing slow and deep.

Breathe in through your nose nice and deeply, aim for 7 seconds and then out through your mouth for 11 seconds, and repeat the exercise five times (it brings more oxygen to your blood and slows down the heart rate).

If you can't quite manage the 7/11 seconds at first, don't worry, most people don't – just keep going, noticing all the while what you need to do, and what adjustments are needed in order to reach the target.

As you start to feel the sensation ebb away, congratulate yourself and reassure yourself that you are fine. You may feel a bit fluffy or lightheaded, and wiped out temporarily as the adrenalin that's been fuelling the anxiety eases off – this won't last long, don't worry.

It can be helpful to have an SOS buddy, someone to call should you ever feel a panic attack coming on. You can even train them to do the breathing steps with you to help guide you through the panic attack, calming you down.

Sip a glass of water to replenish your parched mouth, and carefully and gradually resume whatever you feel comfortable doing, as and when you feel ready.

Well done! Give yourself a big pat on the back and use this technique any time you might feel a bit anxious or panicky.

So there you go, that's how to spot and cope with a panic attack. Now it's time to take a look at one of the major causes of anxiety for parents of newborns: sleep – how lack of it causes anxiety, and how anxiety about how to get it in turn makes you less able to sleep...

Clock watching – will I EVER sleep again?

I think we're all agreed that the single most difficult part of parenthood is adjusting to the lack of sleep. I say 'adjusting', I don't think we ever really fully do that – we just get used to feeling like a jet-lagged mess. Or is that just me?

Before your baby comes along, it's one of the main things you'll hear – 'ooh you better get some sleep now, you can kiss goodbye to sleep once the baby is here'. Thanks for that! My anxiety has always been triggered by sleep deprivation, so you can imagine my fear at knowing that once I had a newborn all bets were off. I honestly worried about this part of being a mum more than anything else before the birth, and it made enjoying the last stages of pregnancy hard.

It's reckoned that a newborn baby should feed (breast or formula) at least eight times in every 24 hours, and there's no doubt about it – mums who breastfeed report that it feels as if the baby is permanently on the boob. Apparently you 'can never overfeed a breast-fed baby', and as the milk production comes in and settles down, the feeding pattern often gradually establishes. There is a belief, supported by several studies that formula-fed babies seem to sleep better/longer. The reason for this is that breast milk is easier to digest than formula milk, meaning breast-fed babies' tummies will be empty more quickly and they need feeding more frequently.

The breast vs formula debate is such a hot topic, and could take up an entire book, so I'll not delve much into it here, but suffice it to say, whichever method you use to feed your baby comes with its own set of challenges. Breastfeeding can be less of a faff in that you can just pick the baby up and help it to latch on, which will usually soothe crying instantly. However, you and your baby getting the hang of breastfeeding in the first place is a whole other story. Breast-fed babies also might wake more regularly and you can't ever tell how much s/he's had. On the other hand, bottle feeders have to go through the making up a bottle charade – sterilising, measuring, mixing, warming, and trying to pacify a starving screaming baby during the whole annoying process – but might just be blessed with a few more precious hours' sleep. Overall, when it comes to feeding and sleep, breastfeeding mums tend to be up more in the night, but it really is horses for courses, and as we know, each baby is different, and there's just no way of knowing how it will turn out.

So, taking into account the fact that we spend around one-third of our day pumping milk into our little ones, add in settling them afterwards (which can take up an hour), and changing nappies – sometimes as many as 12 a day – it's little wonder there's sod all time left for the simplest essentials in life – such as eating, washing and sleeping! And that's if you only have one baby – it all gets a whole lot more challenging with multiples and if you have other little people to care for, too.

Once my baby was here, as predicted, my mind was so wired it was playing havoc with my anxiety and therefore with my sleep – so even when I tried to shut my eyes and catch 40 winks in those brief moments, I couldn't. My body and mind were on overdrive!

'The early feeding stage was hard, particularly the pressure and loneliness that only I could do it. I would look at my sleeping husband with seething resentment that he didn't have to get up (again) to have his nipples gnawed on for the umpteenth time that day.'

Natalie – mum to Finnegan, aged 19 months

How many times have you heard, 'sleep when baby sleeps'? Midwives, well-meaning relatives – I must have had it said to me dozens of times – and it's sensible advice. Some new parents are able to do this quite easily, but for a lot of us it's simply impossible. If you're feeling anxious, stressed and pressured the last thing you feel able to do is lay down and doze off into a blissful power nap.

Every time I tried to snooze all I could think of was 'when's the next feed?' I'd stick my finger under the baby's nose to check he was still breathing, like every 10 minutes, often accidentally waking him in my panic. Each time he made a noise a shot of anxiety would course through me as I scrambled to check he hadn't choked or suffocated in the Moses basket. I would hallucinate and imagine I could hear babies crying, and I would feel my heart going like the clappers as though I'd just done a 100m sprint. Sleep was not my friend. It became my nemesis as I desperately tried to claw some back. But when you're in a heightened state of post-natal anxiety with a lovely side order of birth trauma thrown in, a relaxing rest was not going to be easy to come by.

Having switched from breastfeeding to bottle feeding by day nine, I could rely on my other half for at least *some* of the feeds. The downside was that, as a result, clock watching became a thing in our household – as it is for most people, whether breastfeeding or bottle feeding. We lived and breathed by the digital clock on our bedside table and we would genuinely feel like we'd hit the jackpot if we managed to claw back another hour of sacred sleep thanks to a satisfied milk-drunk baby. Because we were bottle feeding and could share the job, hubby and I devised a system  and called it 'survival mode'. I would go to bed at 8pm and attempt to sleep until the 2am feed, when Enzo would naturally wake starving hungry (we NEVER woke him for a feed! We couldn't face the unpredictable aftermath). Hubby would stay up and do the 11pm feed and then come to bed, where he would get to sleep til hopefully 6am.

Now of course our little bundle was never this predictable, I know some people swear by a strict 'Gina Ford' style routine where you wake baby for feeds, but we decided to just go with the flow and were led by him and his natural waking/feeding/settling pattern, so this plan really was just a template – the reality was some nights Enzo would settle fairly easily post feed (these nights we felt giddy with triumph), other nights he'd scream the house down with colic for two hours – is there anything more draining to attempt to soothe! When this happens, you just have to accept that your baby needs you, although it's worth trying everything to make them more comfortable – feeding, burping, rubbing their tummy, clean nappy, taking off all their clothes and checking them over (if, for example, their dried umbilical cord has fallen off, it could be scratching them, or a label could be sticking in). If it all gets too much and you feel angry, just put them down in their Moses basket or cot so they are safe and take a few minutes to calm down and take some deep breaths, using the opportunity to make a drink, stroke the cats, cry at your partner, scream into a cushion....

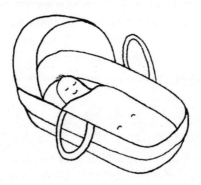

And when we hit the teething phase it was a whole new kettle of fish as the waking every two hours in the night started up again. The husband and I were passing ships – we still are depending on whether or not we're in a teething phase – and in those early days they felt never-ending. I have to say, though, that allowing each other a turn off when possible, did, and does, help to keep our bickering, competitive tiredness and general irritability to a minimum.

Going solo

I was really nervous when my other half went back to work. I would watch that clock like a hawk, waiting for the moment when I knew hubby was due home, when I could get some help and not feel so darn responsible – I struggled to be alone with my little boy in those first few weeks, which makes me sad in one way but also highlights how scary it can feel to suddenly be in charge of a little being. I didn't feel well enough to care for him and I had weird thoughts peppering my mind, such as 'what if I drop him?'

I particularly remember one cold November evening standing at the front door clutching a howling Enzo who was embracing the colic witching hour of screaming from 6–8pm each night, *willing* my other half to walk through the door. When he did I have never been more relieved and he could clearly see I was as distressed as our son. In five minutes he had calmed both of us down and restored our little home to something resembling peace and quiet.

I am so fortunate to have a partner to support me on the off days and pick me up when it all gets too much (I do the same in return of course), so I am in complete and utter awe of parents who go it alone. Whether it's through choice or circumstance, single parenting is without a doubt one of the most admirable things, I think, ever. You're incredible and I take my hat off to you all.

Breaking Point   S.O.S

The night watch is a lonely old time, when your mood is likely to be low and everything can feel like too much. If you are facing some nights where your partner is unable to help, or away, there are some things you can try to make those dreaded night feeds a little more appealing:

IF YOU HAVE a mum pal or even a new mum friendship group, get a WhatsApp group chat going – a lot of mums say this is a total lifeline at 2am when you feel tired and alone feeding your baby on the sofa or in the spare room so as not to wake your partner. It can serve as a source of chat, comfort and support.

STOCK UP ON your favourite magazines, books (and not a baby one for a change!) boxsets, Netflix series, podcasts, or record something from earlier in the day you didn't get a chance to watch or listen to. See the night feeds as a chance to catch up on something enjoyable for you.

ASK A MOTHER/IN-LAW to come round for a night or two to help with the night feeds so you can get some chunks of catch-up sleep. Look into expressing breast milk into a bottle, or combination feeding, to help you out.

CATCH UP ON SLEEP, or just have a rest, in the day by asking a relative or friend to take the baby out in the pram, along with any other children, for a good hour-long walk – you're more likely to relax and rest if you can't hear or see the baby for a short while.

> *'I used to be scared of checking on my son while he was asleep. I would sneak peaks from the doorway, or creep in and out without touching him. I was worried he would wake and be scared of me. And of course, as a result, I wasn't sleeping when I should have been. It seems crazy now!'*
>
> **Erin – adoptive mum to Zach, aged 17 months**

Routine routine routine

'Are they in a routine yet?' It's a question you'll hear a lot. From the moment your baby arrives the pressure is on to get this ticking time bomb on to a timetable. The books and experts are full of promises if you do things 'their way'... Gina Ford, Heidi Murkoff, Tracy Hogg... all promise tranquility and perfect baby bliss in record time, and claim to have the 'recipe for routine'. The problem is, they can also serve as a massive anxiety trigger if you don't seem to be able to get it right, or indeed it may turn you into an insecure mess if you decide to shun their way and do your own thing – especially when you are already sleep deprived and feeling anxious about the whole thing.

So what does 'routine' actually mean? Lots of us are led to believe that the ideal scenario is to have a baby whose day-to-day behaviour and activities are so well timed you could set your watch by them. Feeding, sleeping, bathing, tummy time... the obsession with getting a baby into a routine is something that many parents find themselves trapped in. And why do we do it to ourselves? Haven't we put enough pressure on our already frazzled nerves?

We haven't slept in weeks, we are fumbling through each day in a haze of poo, leaky boobs and sanitary pads, and if that weren't stressful enough our newborn (who doesn't know what they're doing either, just to be clear), is supposed to be in some kind of regimented schedule.

Obviously it would be great to get a good night's sleep once in a while. But I know one thing for sure: the more pressure and subsequent anxiety you place on yourself, the further away from this Holy Grail you're likely to be. I remember a friend of a friend telling me that she'd got her son into a routine from four days old – four days old (!!). I'm hoping she was exaggerating wildly – as how anyone can stick to any sort of pattern in the first few weeks is beyond me. If it IS doable though, please feel free to teach me your ways and I will happily eat my words.

One of the most sensible things I did in the first few weeks was give the proverbial middle finger to even *thinking* of trying to establish any kind of routine. I was just too knackered and the baby was in no mood to embrace it either – having only just been yanked out of his snug home of nine months and into the big bad world he didn't know his arse from his elbow any more than I did!

In an ideal world I'm the kind of person who thrives on schedules and routine, but I knew that if I put pressure on myself to adhere to any kind of pattern in the first few weeks I would come unstuck. I'm not quite sure where this smart self-preservation came from, but I'm so pleased that I just allowed things to 'be' for as long as was necessary. We existed in our little baby bubble for weeks, and just getting through each day feeling grateful that we were all still alive and kicking was enough.

BATH → MILK → BEDTIME

Some people like to introduce the 'bath, milk, bedtime' routine from the beginning – in fact when I interviewed parents more people than I thought confirmed that they tried to establish this from the get-go, with lots admitting this was more for their own sanity to mark the end of surviving another 24 hours. I agree, it's a lovely part of the day, and something we started doing properly from about 12 weeks onwards when *I* felt able to, and once the baby had also got to grips a little more with the difference between day and night time. When I was ready, like my pals, it also served as a daily milestone to tick off and helped to increase my (extremely lacking) positivity.

Feeding and sleeping, when it comes to routines, is a hot topic. Do you feed on demand, or do you stick to every two hours? And that's just a couple of the divisive baby issues you're confronted with as a new parent. We had them all – should we swaddle? Cot or co-sleeping? Do we adopt the self-soothing, controlled crying methods or just rock baby to sleep whenever and however? To dummy or not dummy? It's overwhelming. Suddenly every decision takes on a whole new level of importance and everyone seems to have an opinion. And all it serves to do is breed feelings of anxiety and low self-esteem.

That's not to say of course that imposing a routine of any kind isn't right for some people, especially if you have older children who have to be fed at certain times, dressed and cared for, got to school/nursery, given a little of your undivided attention etc. And that's before you list all the household chores that still need to be done! Sometimes, undoubtedly, the baby being in some sort of a routine is a godsend that allows you to plan a tiny window of me time that first-time mothers can just take whenever the baby is asleep. The point is, it's important to do what you feel is right for you and your family and not to feel pressurised by books, the media or other parents into doing something that you are uncomfortable with.

My top tip, then, is to trust your instincts, be kind to yourself and just go with the flow. Remind yourself frequently that's it's not a competition and there is *no exam at the end*, just do whatever works for you and your baby and your family, and *sod everyone else and their well-meant advice*. Take it all with a pinch of salt and trust that YOU are your child's parent, and as long as you have their best interests at heart, you really won't go far wrong. Now, and in the future, it also helps if you adopt a 'this too shall pass' attitude, viewing each of the blips and challenges that raising children brings, whatever their age, as something that probably won't last forever. In fact, many people find it helpful to stick a note on their fridge door saying 'it's just a phase!!' to serve as a reminder that helps to bring a little perspective to a trying situation.

'Routines are great! But they are
also a pressure... finding one that works for you
and one that allows you to have a life. Up until my
daughter was nine months old I found this a constant
struggle. Especially when travelling and taking
her to babysitters/grandparents.'

Samantha – mum to Delilah, aged 14 months

Going like the clappers

I never knew I could multitask *quite* like I can now! I inherited my mother's genes in that I can juggle several things at once, but it came into its own once I'd become a mum. Oh my goodness, doesn't becoming a parent mean you have your fingers (and whole hands and feet at times) in a lot of pies?!

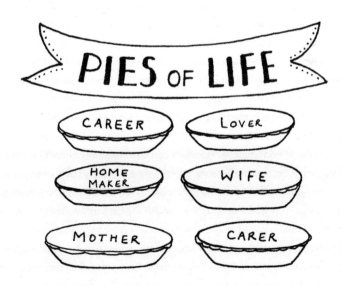

> *'I know that care for my
> appearance changed in the first six months
> or so after having my two, ie no make-up, clothes
> that made it easy to breastfeed and didn't need ironing,
> hair tied up as no time to wash or straighten it. I felt like a
> bedraggled mum and in fact it didn't really bother me – it's
> almost as if I was OK with becoming that mum whose
> appearance reflected the state of my life!'*
>
> **Lizzie – mum to James and Abby**

From the moment I gave birth to Enzo everything suddenly had to be done on turbo mode. Washing, eating, sleeping... if I managed it at all it was done at super-high speed. Part of this was due to the anxiety and OCD esque behaviour which can become part and parcel of the general crappiness I was experiencing. I just HAD to do certain things or I couldn't relax in the slightest.

Everyone tells you to just ignore the cleaning and the washing in the early months, but for me, as it was something I was so on top of *before* having the baby, I just couldn't contemplate living in a pigsty – not even for a day. One of my coping methods for my anxiety has always been to live in as tidy and de-cluttered a place as possible. My surroundings are representative of my mood, mess fuels my stress, so a clean and tidy home helps me to feel more relaxed and chilled. But faced with a newborn baby, feeling like death warmed up, I needed to face facts – I had to let some things go, namely my obsession for whipping out the Cillit Bang at every chance I got.

Some people will no doubt think I'm a bit odd. I've lost count of the number of mum friends telling me how much they relished the early days of parenthood – happily sitting among their own mess and chaos, clothes draped over radiators, nappy changing paraphernalia on every surface – far more interested in paying attention to their new baby.

The thing is, I wanted to be able to do this, too. Some stuff I did manage to ease up on (mainly the Cillit Banging as it wasn't advisable to have the new baby inhaling potentially harmful fumes). I wished I could turn a blind eye to the overflowing washing basket and kitchen sink, but as much as I tried, the moment the baby dozed off, instead of snoozing myself I'd be whizzing around the house like a tornado throwing washes in the machine, sterilising bottles, and making sure the nursery was spotless.

Eating well

There's no doubt that the urge to eat an entire box of chocolate biscuits when you are up for the umpteenth time during the night and are pumping out a gazillion gallons of milk every day is very strong, but now more than ever before it's really important that you eat nutritious food to help your body to recover and to make high-quality milk, if you are breastfeeding. High-sugar and processed foods may be very convenient and comforting, but they cause wild blood-sugar spikes that will ultimately make you feel worse, so try to also include filling fibre-rich foods such as wholemeal bread, fruit, vegetables, pulses and cereals (these will also help with the old constipation if you are on iron supplements), along with lean protein, plenty of calcium and other nutrient-dense foods such as eggs, nuts and seeds. It may be an idea to keep a stash of trail mix, for instance, in your breastfeeding zone, along with big bottles of water to keep you hydrated.

Be aware that there's (yet another) list of foods you are advised to avoid if you are breastfeeding, so make sure your health visitor explains these to you or look them up online.

A final tip: instead of reaching for the Cillit Bang and going on an obsessive cleaning spree while your baby naps, use the time instead to batch cook a load of tasty, nutritious food you can then reheat easily for yourself and your family. Or, if this seems too much, just chop up some vegetables, fruit and cheese and put them in airtight containers in the fridge ready to grab when you are starving and your baby is awake. Hard-boiled eggs can also be cooked in batches, peeled (it's nigh-on impossible to peel an egg one handed while holding a baby!) and stashed away in the fridge.

The one thing I should have been doing in those precious moments when the baby was asleep, if not sleeping myself (no chance), was fuelling my tired body by eating lots of good, nutritious food. And here's the other bugger about anxiety and stress – I was in such a state that I just couldn't physically eat. And when I say I couldn't eat, I mean I genuinely couldn't swallow anything unless it was liquid. My swallowing function was temporarily affected as a side effect of my anxiety. My health visitor was quite rightly concerned, but no one really knew what to suggest. It seems that most new mothers are starving hungry – their bodies are so busy producing breast milk and refuelling post labour. It worried everyone. If it hadn't been for my loving husband persuading me to drink meal replacement supplements full of the good stuff (carbs and proteins), I would have been in a dire situation indeed. Thankfully, the medication started to kick in after a few days, gradually allowing my anxiety to ease and therefore my ability to physically eat increase, and a week or two later I had managed to regain something of a 'normal' appetite – the relief was huge!

So what with the self-inflicted household tasks, attempting a daily 75-second (if I was lucky) shower – after eight hours of night sweats, those lovely releasing hormones made me smell like a sewer each morning – and of course looking after my colicky baby boy, it was no wonder I wasn't exactly enjoying the early days of motherhood. Time is always against you as a parent of a newborn, especially if you have other children, and it's the simple things in life that we find ourselves craving, such as having an actual *hot* cup of tea, replying to a week-old text, and the ultimate 'treat' – going to the loo in peace.

'We tried to take it in turns, but even now there is definitely a sense of resentment or "it's your turn" when she wakes up in the night. Everything changed – not for better or worse, but it all changed. I think the best way of getting through it all was laughing and communicating.'

Kim – mum to Florence, aged nine months

Breaking Point

S.O.S

TAKE A MOMENT each day to STOP. Keeping up with obsessions such as cleaning and routine can take its toll and serves to fuel any anxiety. Remove yourself from the house if you have to, to ensure you're not tempted to do 'just one more thing'. If it means you take your older children to a cafe or a friend's house instead of trying to make them a meal yourself, so be it – you can't always do it all.

USE THIS MOMENT to *enjoy* your baby. Perhaps go for a walk, practise some 'tummy time' or playing on the floor mat, go to the supermarket and push baby round, talking all the time as you shop. Whatever you do, focus on your baby. It's great bonding time and breaks any compulsion to keep doing stuff, and helps you to just slow down.

THE BEST WAY to break OCD-type anxiety is to break the compulsion. It takes time but it's worth it in the long run so find a helpful distraction to take your mind and attention elsewhere.

Dr Reetta says...

Getting to know your baby When there's a baby in the house the days may seem chaotic and unpredictable, and you may feel you are 'doing nothing'. However, 'doing nothing' is part of getting to know each other and although it may be hard to put into words what you are doing all day, you are certainly not 'doing nothing'. Your senses are on high alert and you are responsible for a baby who you are learning to understand. You are working out what your baby seems to want and need – apart from fulfilling their basic requirements of feeding, sleeping and nappy changes – and they will mainly want to be in your company. You are developing as a parent and working out what parenting method or style works for you and your baby. You will probably find yourself thinking whether you are being a 'good mother' or 'good father' and making choices according to what you believe a 'good' parent would do.

What this 'goodness' looks like for each family will vary. It sounds like Anna was following her baby's lead with feeding and sleeping rather than being parent-led and imposing strict routines. This means she was responding to her baby's needs, which would have helped him to feel secure. Anna was also looking after her own well-being. After ensuring the safety and other basic needs of your baby have been met, the most important things to offer to a baby are your love and attention. In the early months, this is largely about non-verbal communication of empathy, warmth and understanding through tone of voice, facial expressions and touch. Later on it also includes talking about feelings and how to express and manage them. A parent who is *looking after themselves* and is able to manage their *own* emotions, is more able to look after their baby.

Top tips for getting to know your baby and dealing with sleep

1. Every day, spend some time just watching your baby. Babies are very social and have an innate need and capacity to communicate. Give eye contact. Learn about what state of alertness (sleep, drowsy, alert, crying/fussy) they are in and watch for signs that they about to change their behaviour. See if you can work out what clues your baby gives you for wanting to play, or when they want some quiet time, so you learn when they are in the mood for communicating and/or playing. Over time, you'll learn to 'read' your baby and how to comfort them. Most importantly, these moments are ideal for bonding and just being together.

2. As Anna describes, sleep deprivation is a common trigger for anxiety. When you are anxious, it is even more difficult to get a good night's sleep. Whichever came first, do have a think about whether there is a way to get a little more sleep and rest. During the day when your baby sleeps, if you can't or don't want to sleep, then give yourself permission to *rest* occasionally – value and prioritise that time. If you can nap, just a 30-minute snooze is thought to have a positive impact on your health and well-being. Ask for help with getting sleep – what Anna and her husband did with the 'milk shifts' is a good example of how a partner can really make a big impact on how much sleep you can get.

3. You have probably heard a lot of conflicting advice about how to get your baby to sleep. Rather than going for a one-size-fits-all approach, as all families and babies are different, first educate yourself about baby sleep, including sleep cycles – see a summary article on 'understanding your baby's sleep' here: https://www.babycentre.co.uk/a558727/understanding-your-babys-sleep. You will learn that an adult sleep cycle lasts about 90 minutes, whereas a baby's sleep cycle lasts around 45-50 minutes, and that it's normal for babies to wake as they transition between sleep cycles (every hour or so!). Second, think about your baby, you and your circumstances – what would work best for you as an individual family? Third, over some weeks or months (rather than days), there are gentle principles that can help you to teach your baby to fall asleep, without your help, and without traumatising them, or you!

Working on 'falling asleep' is important because when your baby wakes at night, they are likely to need whatever you did to get them to sleep in the first place (sleep associations) to help them settle down again. If this is you, and a breast, then this may be a problem further down the line. If you instead help your baby to go to sleep in a situation that is the same as the one they will find themselves in when they wake up between sleep cycles, they should be able to go back to sleep without you. Here are three ideas – if any of these sound like something you want to learn more about, go to www. ahaparenting.com for further reading (the editor of the website, Dr Laura Markham, is a clinical psychologist and a mum – I often use her articles when working with parents).

The three ideas are:

1 Wake your baby slightly before you put them down to sleep;
2 Gradually work on breaking the association between feeding and sleep;
3 Gradually support your baby to fall asleep in their cot or while still in your arms, rather than while being rocked.

If you do decide to work on your baby's sleep, whatever you do, it will require energy and commitment – and it may be sleep depriving and demanding. No approach will produce quick results (or if it does, it may not last or is less than ideal for your baby's well-being). The topic of baby sleep is a tough one and sometimes it is about adapting your expectations and going with a 'this too shall pass' attitude. Parents do often report that they get better at coping with the sleepless nights (in the early weeks and months it can feel impossible). And even the experts have difficulty – it's important to share with you that I am writing this as a clinical psychologist and someone who gives clients advice on sleep – and a mum to two little girls who kept us awake in the nights until they were toddlers!

5
THE KNOW IT ALLS

The 'sit, smile and nod through
gritted teeth' feeling

 *Everybody knows how to raise
children, except the people
that have them.*

P.J. O'Rourke

Baby steps...

PRACTISE selective hearing. Some people have no filter and will say whatever they want regardless of how it might come across. If someone says something that upsets or annoys you, take a deep breath, pretend not to have heard, and swiftly change the subject.

DON'T FEEL the need to justify *your* parenting technique and preferences. Your baby is *your* child, and everyone is entitled to make whatever choices they like.

TAKE SOCIAL MEDIA with a pinch of salt. Competitive parenting is a 'thing' but look through (or even better ignore) the perfect-parent posts, and remind yourself that you know your baby better than anyone.

Public property

There's no doubt about it, the second you get pregnant *everyone* has an opinion. Family, friends, random strangers in the street... the minute a baby is on the horizon, pretty much everyone will a) suddenly think they're experts, and b) give you bucket-loads of 'advice', whether you want to hear it or not.

Family members will bang on about how you should do this, shouldn't do that, and how 'in *my* day blah blah...', friends will encourage you to follow their lead and 'take this supplement' or 'sign up for that class', and I distinctly remember a rather over-zealous fellow mum-to-be next to me in the antenatal clinic (whom I'd never met before!) telling me that I 'needed to give myself a perineum massage otherwise I'd have a damaged vagina forever!' Great. I *really* could have done without the pressure and anxiety this one comment induced in my 38-week-pregnant self. I was already pretty sure my nethers were going to take a bit of a pummelling in any case – I certainly didn't need 'smug mother of four' to unnecessarily highlight it, even though doing this most unglamorous of massage can help prevent tearing.

It genuinely never fails to amaze me that people think it is acceptable to comment and heap advice on new parents – as if it isn't enough of a headf**k as it is. Fair enough if the advice has been asked for but it seems that parenting opens the floodgates to a free-for-all advice deluge. Us Brits might be known for being over-polite and reserved, but for new mums and dads this doesn't seem to apply.

So many of us parents feel daily guilt and pressure about whether we're doing it right, and the last thing we need is some Know It All preaching about *how* and *what* we should be doing. From day one of pregnancy I felt the heat... Already suffering an unhealthy dose of prenatal anxiety, I just couldn't rationally deal with the Know It All brigade. Hindsight is a wonderful thing, and I realise a lot of my anxiety was down to the sheer insecurity about the unknown I was dealing with on a day-to-day basis. To say I was 'snippy' at any unwanted advice would be an understatement... I positively prickled with annoyance at some of it.

One scenario in particular comes to mind. A family friend knew I wasn't enjoying parts of my pregnancy, and their superbly unhelpful advice (passed on via my mum – I think she thought it might have been helpful in that 'we've all been there' kind of way – it wasn't) was 'just tell her to get over it and get on with it'.

Now, I *know* this comment was intended as a light-hearted quip, designed to give to me some helpful perspective, but to my hormonal frazzled mind, all I heard was 'Anna, you're being a hypochondriac, no one cares how you're feeling and basically (wo)man up'. This only served to fuel my anxiety even more – 'if other mums can get on with it and deal with their feelings, then I must be a struggling failure!' – is all I got out of that exchange.

Once my baby arrived the advice giving ramped up even more. I had to adopt an invisible shield to fend off the onslaught.

Activity alert

Let it go

I'm a big fan of using effective breathing to keep anxiety at bay.
It sounds so simple, yet isn't it often the simplest of things we find the
hardest to do? This activity is so easy, but a really effective way of letting any
pangs of panic or anxiety go.

Unwanted opinions or conflicting advice causing you stress? We're going
to breathe it out bit by bit until it's gone.

Take a nice slow and gentle deep breath through your nose ensuring you fill
your tummy with 'air' so it bulges out... then as you exhale through your
mouth slowly, allowing your tummy to deflate gradually with each number,
you're going to quietly say, or think, the numbers 1–10.

These numbers each represent any niggles, negativity, pent-up frustration or
unwanted advice you want to rid your mind of.

Keep the outward breath continuous, and with each passing number
visualise and imagine each of them floating away on a cloud into obscurity
and irrelevance.

Once you've reached 10... all your breath calmly exhaled... as you breathe
back in imagine all you're breathing in is fresh, crisp, clean air – a
wonderfully clear blank canvas in your mind, full of positivity and calming
clarity.

Any time someone says something that bugs you, or you feel yourself
doubting your own ability, allow yourself to breathe out all the negative
thoughts and feelings, leaving you feeling calm and back in control.

Boob or bottle – that is the question?

I can see you now, readying yourself for the battleground of this age-old, and often highly subjective, debate. Since the dawn of time (well, since formula and bottle feeding were invented) never has there been a more emotive topic of debate among new parents. And it isn't just a woman thing either, it's a BIG deal for dads, too, with many of them having extremely strong feelings about what they do/don't feel is appropriate for their child.

Usually, then, because men obviously can't breastfeed they simply have to accept whatever a mother is or isn't capable of doing or simply how *they* choose to feed their child. This fact can breed a heck of a lot of hidden parenting anxiety, and a feeling of a lack of control, in new dads (more of this in chapter 8) and lead to discord.

For many, though, it's ultimately down to the mother to decide how best to feed her child – whether through personal preference or for medical reasons that make breastfeeding impossible, such as the baby having a tongue tie, being unable to latch on, being seriously underweight, or one of multiples that the mother can't keep up with, or the mother having issues with milk supply, chronic mastitis or other physical issues, or having to take medication – and the men are more than happy to go along with it. I know plenty of women who have adamantly refused to breastfeed their children, preferring to opt for formula from day one, and I equally know lots of ladies who have exclusively breastfed their babies for years, having never grappled with a steriliser or silicone teat in their lives. For what my lowly little opinion is worth, I believe it is nobody's business other than those involved – ie the mum, dad (if applicable) and baby.

It's good to talk

One mum told me that her partner was extremely keen on their daughter being breastfed. The mum really struggled to make it work for her, but she kept going because of the (unintentional) pressure the dad put on her. With the benefit of hindsight she says she wishes she had spoken up at the time and conveyed HER wishes more – after all it was her body – but she felt guilty that it was his desire and he was unable to do it himself. Next time round she has vowed she is going straight to formula and the bottle and, after a proper discussion and airing of feelings, her partner has understood her choice.

Feeding your baby is a highly personal and emotional experience. No matter which option you end up with, both have their benefits and challenges. And remember, it's *your* body and baby. Although sometimes you wouldn't think it: I have lost count of how many times I have been made to feel like crap and the worst mum in the world ever after some cretin's ill-thought-out opinion on how I should feed my baby has touched a nerve.

'As soon as I decided to formula feed it was like a major weight had been lifted off my shoulders. Even though there are a lot of health care professionals who remain positive about formula feeding there are a few that are quite judgemental, which is really hard.'

Farrah – mum to Luca

The main reason I chose to give up breastfeeding and instead opted for the bottle and formula was because of my medication. I say I 'chose', but to be honest it was a choice I *had* to make, but not one I really wanted to – it had to happen to stabilise my tattered new mummy mental health.

I recognised the black cloud of depression and anxiety just days after having Enzo, and I knew I needed to do something about my mental health quick smart before I went even further down an unpleasant route. Studies are ongoing, but in general doctors warn against taking certain anti-depressants while breastfeeding as the medication can be transferred, albeit in small doses, to the baby via the breast milk. Some anti-depressants are deemed 'safer' than others, such as Sertraline and Paroxetine, which allegedly carry less dosage through the milk, but other medications such as Citalopram and Fluoxetine carry a much higher level, which some studies suggest can lead to irritability, decreased feeding and sleep problems for the baby. Always chat through the options with your doctor, so you can make an informed decision on whether medication is a route for you or not.

> *'I'd been feeling so emotional for weeks after giving birth, and just felt so resentful towards my son for making me feel like this. When my GP prescribed me anti-depressants I was at my lowest ebb and I really felt I needed something to help. After a couple of weeks things started to feel less rubbish and I gradually started to enjoy the rewarding parts of motherhood.'*
>
> **Catrina – mum to Sonny, aged 12 months**

I started on Sertraline. When it wasn't working and I changed to Citalopram and also took a slightly higher dose – I erred on the side of caution (of course I did, I was an anxious guilt-ridden mess) – I decided the best option, for me, was not to risk any 'bad stuff' reaching my baby at all. So after nine days of feeding Enzo myself, I packed up my boobs, said goodbye to the breastfeeding circus, and cracked open the formula. A very emotional decision, and one I was pretty tetchy about as I felt the need to explain to everyone why I wasn't feeding my son myself any more – and that meant fessing up to the fact I was on anti-anxiety and anti-depressant medication. If that wasn't a hot topic of gossip among other mums I don't know what was! The question 'are you breastfeeding?' used to fill me with dread.

It didn't help that my husband was a bit miffed that his son wasn't going to be getting any more of the 'good stuff' from mum – yet another bone of contention and an anxiety-fuelling issue, and we had many a conversation about how this might work going forwards. I'm so pleased and proud that my husband agrees now that it was absolutely the right decision for us all, especially the baby as he needed a well mother. But at the time I know my other half felt very disappointed that, in his opinion, his precious son wasn't going to be getting all the nutrients and nourishment from my milk (he is a nutrition specialist after all, so the more natural the food source the better!) – and that made me feel so guilty. Although he initially would have preferred breast milk, he now agrees that overall health and bonding for mother and baby is what is key, and the milk source is not always the be all and end all. It also helped *him* bond with the baby as he got to join in with feeds, so all in all bottle feeding has been a positive experience for us.

> 'I struggled to breastfeed
> and the pressure from others (including
> family) was quite overwhelming. Eventually after
> four days of trying my sympathetic partner said
> "why don't we try her on formula" - the fact that
> I knew he was supporting me, even though
> formula wasn't the original plan, was a major relief.'
>
> **Bronwen – mum to a little girl**

A lot of new mums also find it bloody hard to breastfeed at all! Even if it's their decision to give breastfeeding a go, it annoyingly doesn't always work out. I've lost count of the number of friends who have really struggled to breastfeed and regard it as 'the hardest thing they have ever endured' ... and believe me, these women aren't little princesses scared of breaking a nail – they're hardcore.

What with cracked nipples, slow and painful let-down/milk flow, tongue-tied babies, other latching-on issues, the dreaded mastitis, and the general paraphernalia that breastfeeding can involve, it's no wonder the pushy Know It Alls who insist 'breast is best' have a lot to answer for when it comes to evoking anxiety!

The majority of midwives, health visitors and maternity professionals are very pro breastfeeding, and hey, I'm fully in favour of it too, IF that's what a woman wants to do. But there is a borderline bullying culture that surrounds breastfeeding, even when religious and cultural factors aren't in play, with any mum of a newborn daring to shun or failing to thrive the 'natural way' made to feel uncomfortable and worried they have to justify their choice.

'The big issue in those first few weeks was breastfeeding. Not the actual feeding - which, as mums will tell you but none of the professionals seem to, hurts so so much in such an intimate way - but the feeling of utter failure I felt because of the health visitor's comment: "it will not hurt if you are doing it right."'

Holly – mum to Jack, aged 12 months

I've tried breastfeeding, it's wonderful (sometimes) and feels as though you've hit the jackpot when it goes well and you see your baby's gorgeous little face looking up at you, among the stack of pillows and muslin paraphernalia, as they feed, but it's also messy, fiddly and can be painful to establish, and it's no wonder so many of us find it a huge challenge.

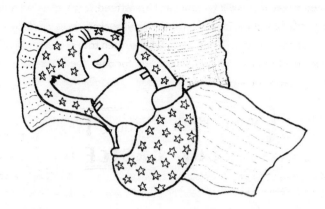

I also found it a very weird thing to suddenly comprehend that my funbags which had up until the point of motherhood served no other purpose than to aid the pleasure of a night of 'sexy time', were now stripped of all sexual status, and were instead solely a feeding machine.

It was more than a little mind-blowing to comprehend to be honest, and it was a slightly terrifying, but weirdly cool and surreal moment when they started leaking milk. And yet the moment the milk is 'in' (again, often not until a day after you give birth, by which point your baby is often fractious and starving hungry – just when you're trying to get the hang of how to feed them), everyone seems to want to have a prod, poke and squeeze. How many times have you heard from new mums, 'my boobs are not my own anymore' ... and it's so true. It seems everyone wants to have a go at yanking your mammaries around in order to get baby latched on and feeding. Everyone has an opinion on how to do it, what they did, how 'so and so' was a natural... the Know It Alls really do go batshit about boobs.

And my goodness if you decide to breastfeed in public... More Know It All opinions! I'm sure you have your own thoughts on the breastfeeding-in-public debate, and here are mine: anyone who gives a mother stick for feeding her child wherever she damn well likes needs to quietly sod off back under the prehistoric rock they've crawled out from. It's hard enough trying to sate a screaming baby under a flannel-sized 'privacy' muslin, with one nipple sprouting a misdirected leak and the other soaking a wet patch into your T-shirt without unwanted opinions, thank you very much.

My advice? Well of course, I'm not going to be a Know It All and infuriate you by giving you any – but all I will do is casually remind you that *you are entitled to do what the heck you like regarding your body.* If you want to breastfeed, great, if you want to but can't breastfeed, don't worry about it, and if you physically balk at the idea of having your tit sucked like a toddler demolishing an ice pop on a hot summer's day, then totally make that call to crack open the formula-and-bottle meal deal for one. Your body, your baby, your choice – and you are doing brilliantly!

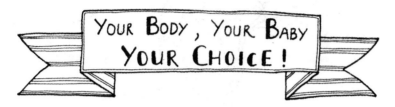

'I overheard a conversation between my in-laws which pretty much questioned why I breastfed. I felt very upset and angry at the lack of understanding and support. I wanted to be congratulated for the hard work I was doing.'

Eliza – mum of two

When all is not so well

Some parents, who in my eyes are Super Heroes, have extra challenges to face such as coping with a child who is unwell, or perhaps dealing with a disability. This can be incredibly worrying and challenging and, in particular, the Know It Alls' sensitivity radar needs to be cranked right up to the 'wind your neck in' setting.

We've all no doubt faced the new-parent anxiety over our baby's first sniffles and fever. It's a highly stressful time as, let's be honest, few of us have a clue what to do or how best to make our child well. My phone bill should just be linked as a permanent direct debit to the NHS 111 service given the amount of times we call for advice! (and FYI these Know It Alls are *extremely* welcome in our household – the people on the end of the phone are an anxious parent's lifeline).

The first time my son got a fever, which coincided with his first lot of jabs (gosh isn't that an un-fun experience), I was terrified that he was going to die. Irrational, probably... but a very real fear, absolutely. *Obviously,* in my head, he had meningitis (he didn't) – every parent's worst nightmare – so each hour I would be shoving the thermometer under his tiny clammy armpit and obsessing over what the temperature reading 'beeps' signified. Fortunately Dr Calpol saved the day (doesn't it always!) and within hours my little boy was back to his normal self.

I'm well aware that baby coughs and colds really are trivial stuff when it comes to what some parents have to endure – in fact I'm sure many would welcome such an easy-fix problem. Babies born with birth defects or disabilities can understandably cause a lot of distress and worry to parents. Nearly a million children in the UK come under the disability category, and this can include physical and mental disabilities, learning disabilities, and disorders on the spectrum such as autism. Sometimes it can take a while to notice all is not as you 'expect' in your child, and in other cases it's apparent from birth that little one has a few challenges ahead.

Mothers and fathers of babies with more complex requirements really do not need unwanted or insensitive 'well-meaning' advice. And it is perfectly natural and understandable for them to withdraw from other parents who seemingly have a 'normal' child – all it takes is one thoughtless comment to completely crush an already struggling parent. But it's vitally important that these parents and children in particular get all the support and empathy they need. Isolating yourself isn't going to help anyone in the long run.

If you're a parent who has a baby or child who is perhaps not well, has complex needs or is facing a challenging road ahead, trust your instincts and get whatever help you feel is appropriate. Support and help is there. The NHS Early Support Programme, the NCT and Mencap all offer support and advice from those specifically trained to know how to help you on the road ahead.

'Watching the other babies at playgroup just highlighted how different my daughter was. She didn't do the normal things the others her age did, like sit up on her own or reach out for toys. It made me feel angry... "why did I have to have a baby that was different?" It's tough and there's a long road ahead, but her smiles remind me that I'm her mummy, and I love her. That's all that matters.'

Sally – mum to Ruby

Health anxiety

In addition to naturally feeling worried about your child's health and well-being, there is a related condition that seems to be getting more common. Health anxiety, or the more old-fashioned, outmoded term, hypochondria, is no laughing matter. For those experiencing it, it is a very real fear of, and/or belief that they are seriously ill, and the day-to-day stress and anxiety it can cause for sufferers is often extremely life restricting. It simply doesn't help the sufferer if someone tells them 'pull yourself together'.

Some people are managing a health condition, which they worry about excessively, others have medically unexplained symptoms such as aches and pains, which they are concerned might be a serious illness. Despite doctors' reassurances people experiencing health anxiety are convinced there is something more sinister lurking, and worries about future health such as 'will I get cancer?' also feel very real.

Health anxiety can be experienced for a number of reasons. You might be a worrier in general, have a pre-disposed anxiety or depressive disorder, or you may have experienced a stressful event that happened to someone close to you, involving illness, or even death. All parents can experience health anxiety due to a number of reasons or triggers – a traumatic birth, coping with a sickly or unwell baby, having experienced a stillbirth in the past, or feelings that they might one day be too ill to look after their child – and therefore irrationally obsess over keeping well.

It's always advisable to pop and see your GP to chat over how you're feeling and any fears you may have relating to you or your baby's health to ensure you get any help or talking therapy support you might benefit from. It's nothing to be embarrassed about, and you're certainly not alone. With the right intervention it's perfectly possible to get any unhelpful feelings of anxiety around your health sorted.

'My father-in-law said, "so what steps are we going to do to stop her from using the comforter?" – erm how about "we" are not going to do anything and "you" need to stop giving your opinion.'

Sam – dad to Charlie, aged 15 months

Breaking Point

STOP FUELLING any anxiety further by actively avoiding any unhelpful triggers. Do NOT Google or research symptoms as it can just unnecessarily ramp up anxiety even more.

INSTEAD OF focusing on things that might seem wrong, turn your attention to what feels good... ie instead of dwelling on aches and pains, take your attention to how good it feels when you breathe in some fresh air, allowing your mind and body to relax.

DISTRACT YOURSELF from any negative thoughts. Negativity will just keep breeding if you don't change the course. Look for, and think of all the positive things in your and your family's lives, and practise being thankful for what IS good.

IF YOU are genuinely concerned about something, go and see your doctor. They will be able to either confirm it is an ailment, and can treat it, or they can reassure you that all is well. Either way, doing this will remove the uncertainty and you may well find that just speaking out loud what's on your mind will make the symptoms disappear!

You say, I say

Differing parenting styles are always going to be an interesting talking point. No one parents the same way – each child and parent and family dynamic is unique, so the chances are that the way we choose to parent will be different to someone else's. And it starts within the home: us mums and dads can each have differing ideals and parenting styles, often influenced by our own childhoods and culture, which can sometimes throw up conflict in an otherwise harmonious relationship, and takes some compromise for it to be resolved.

And oh how the multitude of books, magazines, apps and websites will tell you that 'their' way is best! Some of them have some pretty fab ideas, tips and suggestions, and being the bookworm I am, I scoured pretty much every piece of parenting literature on offer, whereas other friends deliberately ignored everything, preferring to stay in their ignorant bliss (their words not mine). The end result, though, was that I was more confused than I'd been when I started!

There's never a simple answer

A random sample of contradictory advice I remember coming across:

Q Should I swaddle my newborn baby?
A Some advisors say yes – others say let them be free to wriggle.

Q At what age should my baby be in his own room?
A Some resources suggest putting them in their own nursery from six weeks but others such as the NHS guidelines fly the 'only after six months' flag.

Q Do I need a baby movement sensor monitor?
A Some say yes so you can tell if baby stops breathing (!) – others say it'll drive you mad with paranoia.

Q Should I use a special baby bath?
A Some suggest the perfect contraption with built-in water thermometer etc – others say don't bother and just use the actual bath.

Q Should you introduce bottle while breastfeeding early on?
A Some say yes, so the baby gets used to combination feeding, others say don't do it for fear of confusing the baby!

Q When do I start weaning? Should it be baby led or should I do purée?
A Some advice says wait until six months when they can hold their own food and feed themselves, others say if baby seems hungry/interested in food, or if they have very bad reflux and/or colic, you could start at four months by introducing spoon-fed baby rice/purée.

Q Dummies – yes or no?
A Lots agree they're great to pacify a crying/sucky child, others warn it can damage speech or teeth!

Arghhhhh! Is it any wonder we're all running around like headless chickens and panic buying anything and everything from Amazon Prime! And of course the advice changes all the time, too, so what goes for your first baby may not apply the second time round – which just goes to show that sometimes even the experts can get it wrong.

> *'I could certainly have done without the unsolicited opinions from well-meaning fools such as one health visitor who said that bringing the children up bilingually would confuse them. And all that running around the garden would be bad for their joints. What utter nonsense!'*
>
> **Dr Hilary Jones – TV doctor and dad**

So that's the madness online. And then there's the conflicting health professionals' advice. Some suggest weaning at four months, others are adamant that six months is best for baby. Health visitors and midwives, it seems, are a little inconsistent with their advice... I'm sure a lot of this is down to their own individual preferences, but it can be a total and utter head wreck! Particularly for a knackered parent at their wits' end. I lost count of the amount of opinions I had over my son's cradle cap. 'Try massaging in olive oil' said one midwife, 'Don't use oil whatever you do, try brushing it', said another. Essentially, like a lot of advice in life, when it comes to being a parent, you take it with a pinch of salt and basically make up your own mind (incidentally it was a *combination* of the oil/brushing that actually did the trick on my little dude's flakey scalp).

And then we have The Grandparents – cue dramatic thunder and lightning strike! Good lord, is there anything more wearing that the constant barrage of advice the proud new grannies and grandpas want to offer up? Now, I'm lucky, I have a very lovely and unintrusive mother-in-law, and my folks are brilliant and pretty laid back when it comes to their new grandson, too. However, it hasn't stopped my mother in particular trotting out the wretched phrases 'well in MY day...', and 'WE didn't have this new-fangled technology', and 'you lot don't know you're even BORN!'... honestly, the way my mother harps on about rearing children in the 1970s and 1980s (in middle-class rural England) makes it sound as though they were living in a primitive wartime coal bunker!

> *'Visiting the in-laws has been
> so difficult, as it really grates me when
> they think they always know best. I appreciate
> the fact that they've been through it all before,
> but we also know our baby the best.'*
>
> **Hannah – mum to Liliana**

Now, not for one minute am I being an arse about my parents, or indeed anyone else's parents – I genuinely have the best folks in the world, I love them to pieces, and would be screwed without their constant love, support and help. They are also incredible with our son... However, I think we are all agreed that The Grandparents, and family members in general really do often come into their own Know It All glory the moment a new baby joins the clan.

But before we get too ratty and annoyed with our loved ones, let's remind ourselves that it's usually because they care. I often find the best approach is to choose your battles. He's *my* baby so ultimately I will decide how I rear him, but if my mum insists on trussing my boy up in umpteen cardigans in August – 'in case he catches a chill!' – or smothers his post-bath body in a heady mix of nappy cream and talcum powder, I'm not going to give her stick for it. She did it with us, and you know what, my brothers and I have turned out pretty well, so as far as I'm concerned, if it makes her happy then go for your life ma! (just please keep the 'you modern mothers want it all' comments to a minimum if you will).

> *'When I'm with certain
> members of the family, I have to always
> remind myself that I'm her mum and try and
> believe in myself and my ability a bit more.
> Maybe at times the hormones have made me
> feel upset, but you are very sensitive to
> your ability so early on.'*
>
> **Lauren – IVF mum to Dolly**

Right back atcha

This activity is all about standing up for yourself and your feelings, and allowing that inner confidence and self-esteem to grow.

Having a few tried-and-tested responses can be really helpful in politely yet firmly warding off any unwanted opinions, and can really aid in boosting your parenting self-confidence.

Imagine you're standing opposite someone who's about to give you some uninvited advice – perhaps you can imagine a scenario that has already happened, such as someone telling you how best to feed your baby, or how you should be tackling sleep time...

Now, remind yourself of the kind of fabulous parent you are, how you want to bring up your child, what's important to you as a parent, and why you are confident in the choices you make – really go through each point and create an answer.

Take a nice deep breath, hold your head up high, shoulders back. In your mind's eye I want you to imagine looking directly at this person and responding to their comments confidently, knowing and believing in your parenting skills.

Imagine their response and, better still, get some further perspective by removing yourself from the situation to a short distance away from the scene so you can view what's going on from afar – as though you've stepped out of your shoes and are looking back at you, and you're noticing what the conversation looks and sounds like from this disassociated position.

From this vantage point you are able to remove some of the emotion involved in such a conversation, and gain some valuable perspective on how you might handle such a situation in the future.

Perhaps you could arm yourself with even more positivity and think of a few general responses such as 'thank you for your input, but I've made the right choice for me and my baby' or 'it's important that I work out how to do things my way' or 'please respect my decisions' – make sure you believe in what you are saying, and have them ready to use as and when you might need them.

Well done. You know what you're doing – well... we all make it up as we go along I reckon – but it's important that your parenting journey goes the way *you* choose it to.

> *'If I can offer any advice
> I would say never compare yourself
> to any other parent or feel you are not
> doing as good a job. You are doing the best
> you possibly can because you care so much.
> You are unique and brilliant.'*
>
> **Una Healy – pop star and mum of two**

The proud parent

Hopefully there are times when you're able to peek through the monotony of routine and the relentless grizzling, bat off the Know It All advice givers, and notice that actually you're doing something incredible – you're caring for your very own little person. Among all the practical stuff that it requires to care for a child, and dealing with any feelings of insecurity and 'am I doing it right?' concerns, it can be so difficult to just be 'in the moment' and enjoy your baby for what s/he is... yours.

So many mums tell me that they are often so busy keeping up with the day-to-day demands of being a parent, putting the washing on, sorting feeds out etc, making endless bolognese to shovel down the necks of older siblings... that they forget to actually take notice of their baby, and on reflection, wish they had put more of the trivial stuff to one side, ignored a lot of the opinions, and just enjoyed their little one more. There really is nothing more stress-busting for me than hearing my son giggle, or copying me blowing a raspberry while giving me a massive grin. Choose a moment each day to just 'be' with your baby and allow yourself some time away from the mundane slog and Know It Alls to chill and appreciate each other.

How to... appreciate your baby

BEING CLOSE physically can be a really good bonding experience – perhaps try a baby carrier or sling and go for a walk with your little one close to your body. Just sniffing their head and feeling their warmth can trigger the feel-good hormones.

READ A STORY – it doesn't really matter how old your baby is, the act of snuggling up together reading a story helps in enjoying the moment together. It's a great way to just focus on your quality time together.

PLAY COPY-CAT faces – even from a fairly young age of a few weeks, babies love to copy facial expressions – smiling, sticking your tongue out, closing your eyes… whatever your baby's age, give it a try and enjoy the eye-to-eye contact it brings. Show older children how to do this too, so that they can join in and feel involved and really bond with the new kid on the block who is diverting a lot of your attention away from them (how dare it!).

Each day is different. Some days are good, perhaps even thoroughly enjoyable, others are anything but. Recognise what you've achieved, even if that's just changing out of one pair of PJs and into another fresh pair! Appreciate what you enjoy, and what you don't, and embrace the good days and allow the shit ones to come and go… give yourself permission to be OK with that.

Frenemies

And finally in the world of Know It Alls, we have other parents. Now, I have to say that I've been REALLY blessed with my mum friends, new ones and 'already' mum mates. I have been met with minimal Know It All parenting advice and forced opinions, in fact I've had bucket loads of helpful suggestions. You're always going to get one or two eyebrow-raising comments, but hey, that's life.

I was also very lucky to have met a cracking bunch of girls through my NCT and baby clubs' groups. Before I became a mum I was a bit snobby about these sorts of coffee-and-cake gangs since I thought all anyone did at them was prattle on about 'how wonderful little Lily was' and 'isn't Harry handsome' blah blah, and basically made you feel like a bit of an incompetent fool.

Now, I know there are plenty of these types of mums, and that's totally fine with me, I think every parent has the right to gush over their offspring and show off to all and sundry, but I'm a big believer in 'like attracts like', and for me, these keeping up with the Jones'-type parents are just not for me. I've met a few in certain one-off circles and quite frankly the last thing I need is another mother making me feel like crap and comparing and judging my parenting choices. Sod. That.

It really naffs me off when I hear from some mums that they've been met with competitive, judgey behaviour from fellow mums. One lady told me how she felt so rubbish after another mum unhelpfully commented that her son 'seemed a bit behind as he wasn't sitting up yet, and her own son had been doing it for weeks!' – where's the sisterhood there?!

I prefer to stick to what, and who, I know and that is being open, honest, all-inclusive and, above all, friendly to any fellow parent who fancies muddling through this parenting malarkey with me over a glass of wine and no-holds-barred natter. I'll be going into the nerve-wracking business of making new mum friends in the next chapter, but with regards to the Know It Alls, never feel you have to measure yourself against anyone else, or justify your choices. Anyone who questions why you did this? and shouldn't you do that? or just makes you feel a bit rubbish, perhaps just needs to be avoided altogether. No one needs that kind of crap, let alone a new mum.

> 'A lot of people want to give you advice, and I think my problem was that I took it all to heart and personally. When a friend said I shouldn't have the baby in bed with me and he should be sleeping in his cot by himself, I felt awful. I also felt enormous guilt, as I had been very critical of others before I'd become a mum.'
>
> **Katie – mum to Charlie, aged 11 months**

Dr Reetta says...

Trusting yourself and listening to advice

Parenting can be a very personal and emotive topic. The reaction many of us have to advice may be partly because we are reacting to the pressures and unrealistic expectations of today's parenthood, where it often feels impossible to get it 'right'. Modern mothers and fathers tend to want to make their own decisions rather than automatically following family traditions, which sometimes causes tensions. Theories and advice on baby care keep changing, too, so those advice-giving conversations could sometimes be seen as interesting comparisons, rather than anything more. As Anna says, take it as one way to view the situation, then make up your own mind. Sometimes other people are keen to give advice because they feel they have learned from their own 'mistakes' and they want to pass this knowledge on to others. Everyone goes through challenges slightly differently, and as they learned from their 'mistakes', you will learn from yours.

I want to say a few words about being 'good enough' (a concept originating from the work of paediatrician and psychoanalyst D.W. Winnicott) as a parent – something I talk about with all the parents I see in my clinic. This may be a concept you want to think back to when you feel overwhelmed with advice and others' opinions. A 'good enough' parent adapts and responds to the needs of their baby, and is sensitive and empathetic towards them. As the baby grows, the parent allows that there will inevitably be some frustration and experiences that may not be quite what they would wish. Babies will go through times when no matter what you do, you can't settle them. If you can encourage and tolerate all their feelings without becoming *too* overwhelmed (it is normal to find these times upsetting and overwhelming!), you are giving your baby experiences of being soothed and held (emotionally and literally), which will help them self soothe when they are a little older. Being 'good enough' teaches your child that it's OK to feel frustrated and sad at times.

Top tips for dealing with advice from others and trusting your own style

1. If you do want advice from people around you, say so. Some people assume they know what type of help new parents would like, and although it may feel slightly awkward for you to be specific, it could be helpful for everyone involved. Most family and friends who give advice probably mean well and want to help, but perhaps need to be guided to the right direction. Are they engaging in advice giving because they don't know how else to contribute? Similarly, when the roles are reversed, instead of offering advice or opinions to fellow parents, offer a listening ear instead. Be there to think and problem solve with them. Perhaps don't offer advice at all if it hasn't been asked for.

2. After you have done Anna's Activity Alert in chapter 3, 'Who do you think you are', and thought about your values, then think, what would your days look like if you were living by these values? You may have an idealistic image of what you would like life with a baby to look like. What would 'good enough' parenting look like for you? Once you have your 'good enough' image of you as a parent, it is about aiming for all of this a 'good enough' amount of time, rather than *all* the time (this will allow for the unavoidable bad days without you feeling like you are failing). Then trust yourself, especially in those moments when you are receiving unwanted advice.

3. You will find yourself comparing yourself against someone else who is doing 'more' or 'better' sooner than you. This is normal, everyone does it – human beings all compare themselves to others. When you notice this happening, are you only seeing a partial image of this other person? The good and positive aspects of them? Could it be that this person is doing well in this area, but struggling in another? Are you noticing what is going well for *you*, rather than just what aspects you are struggling with? Asking yourself these questions encourages flexible, balanced thinking – a handy tool in any parenting anxiety-management toolkit.

'I'm a strong woman and have my own opinions. I nod politely when given advice, and some has been useful, but I make my own decisions and am not swayed or feel inadequate – I know I can make the best choices for my children.'

Mel – mum of twins

6
FRIENDSHIPS AND RELATIONSHIPS

The 'first day of school' feeling

Friendship ... is born at the moment when one man says to another "What! You too? I thought that no one but myself ..."

C.S Lewis, *The Four Loves,* **1960**

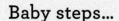
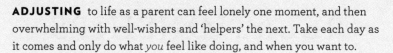

Baby steps...

ADJUSTING to life as a parent can feel lonely one moment, and then overwhelming with well-wishers and 'helpers' the next. Take each day as it comes and only do what *you* feel like doing, and when you want to.

AVOID CLIQUES. For every snooty mum clique, you'll find 10 normal and down-to-earth groups of mums. Never feel you have to compare yourself to any other parent, and do surround yourself with like-minded fellow mums and dads.

A PROBLEM SHARED is a problem halved. Don't bottle up any negative feelings, or let worries and insecurities fester. Be brave and talk about how you feel – you will not be alone in your thoughts and concerns.

New kid on the block

I've always been extremely lucky in that I've had a lot of the same friends since school, and as the only girl in my family (and I used to feel really hard done by not having a sister to nick clothes and make-up from), I'm blessed that along the way and into my early adulthood, I made some very close friends and confidantes who I consider my 'sisters' still today. True friends are worth their weight in gold and I'm blessed to have some of the very best.

So, when faced with my new pregnancy at the grand old age of 35, in my mind, the last thing I thought I needed were any new friends. With the sporadic work life I lead it's often hard enough to keep up with the ones I already have, and yet, faced with the reality that I was going to be a mum, I suddenly felt this intense need to meet and talk to other women in my situation, and compare notes. Lots of my pals have children – in fact I'm one of the last to get sprogged up, but as a new mum to a now 10-month-old I can totally appreciate how even a few months of a baby age gap can make a huge difference between feeling like someone is on your exact wavelength, or not.

I'd always wished I could somehow time it to ensure I had a baby around the same time as one of my friends, someone to hang out with in Mothercare shopping for disgustingly over-priced buggies, and sniggering over breast pumps in John Lewis as we scoffed cake to our hearts' content under the guise of 'needing the energy' (the law for any expecting mum), but of course, things don't quite work that way. I found out I was pregnant in the first week of January 2016 by a bit of a fluke really – I only did the test out of habit and to use up the last one in the box.

So, here I was, in the baby way and I didn't know anyone else who was in the same situation as me – typical. Umpteen godchildren, loads of friends' kids, but nobody pregnant. I was literally the only person I knew having a baby and I craved a 'friend' I could whinge to and get excited and compare growing bumps with. Don't get me wrong, all my friends were incredible and so excited for me, but I don't think there can be a substitute for someone going through such a momentous life change as you at the same time. Having not delved into the 'making new friends' minefield since school some 20 years before, I had no clue where to start – I felt like a right novice. And so I decided to take my other 'already mum' friends' advice, and join the NCT (National Childbirth Trust).

'Another big adjustment for
me was the slowing in the pace of life and the
lack of friends in a similar position. I was the first
among our friends to have a baby, we'd moved to the
countryside two years before I got pregnant, but we had
very few local friends as our social lives and jobs were
still in London. Everyone told me that you meet people
when you've got a baby, and they were right.'

Laura – mum to Saffy, aged 10 months

Making mum mates

It's weird, you do this incredibly grown-up thing by becoming a parent, and yet, for me, I'd never felt more like a kid on the first day of school in my life! It's a surreal feeling knowing that life as you've previously known it is about to become a whirlwind of weigh-in clinics, baby classes and kids' tea parties, and it was one I resisted at first. I think it was a lot to do with being scared about losing my independent working woman status and feeling 'done' in that respect – working in broadcasting and media, never an inviting prospect!

I wanted to meet people embarking on a similar journey to me but, in my narrow-minded head, I didn't want to become one of 'those' people whose day revolved around kids' activities, competing with other mums for acceptance, and consuming vats of caffeine. I had such a weird, misplaced judgement surrounding it and have never liked cliques, so I really worried that this is what I'd be faced with. It turns out I wasn't alone in my apprehension about meeting other mums – pretty much all the women I've spoken to talked of their fears about having to step out of their comfort zone and set foot into the daunting world of new parents.

A lot of mums find joining mum groups, such as coffee mornings, mums and babies groups, buggy fit etc, a really positive experience, but I totally appreciate that there are some who unfortunately don't have quite such an easy transition or feel comfortable mixing with new people. I get it, it's not just about you any more, it's you WITH a baby in tow and that can cause so much extra anxiety, feelings of inadequacy, worries about being judged, and self-consciousness, and all it takes is the wrong comment at the wrong time to knock an already nervous mum right off her stride.

One mum friend spoke of feeling like a bit of a loner and as though she'd missed out on the new friend thing as she'd moved house just weeks before her baby was born. Faced with a new town and new people, she spoke of the nerves she felt at mum and baby clubs and as though everyone was already friends and in groups, so she just wasn't sure where or how she could fit in. Thankfully, she wasn't put off by feeling left out, and with brilliant bravery and insight signed up for a six-week baby massage course at her local Children's Centre – the repetition of going every week with the same parents and babies really helped her confidence to grow, and for her to get to know them, and them her, and by the end of the course she'd got a few fellow mums' phone numbers with plans to meet for coffee.

Breaking Point

DON'T STRESS! Just because you're a new parent doesn't mean you are alone – there will most certainly be others feeling the same as you and wanting a friend. The trick is to find each other.

NEW PALS don't just fall in your lap, you have to go and find them... Be brave and reach out to other parents. Local Sure Start Children's Centres (which offer free or subsidised classes, such as feeding talks, baby massage, baby sensory) and baby drop-in clinics (which each town offers as part of NHS post-natal care) are great places to meet new mums and dads, and your health visitor will be able to recommend local groups, talks and classes you might like to attend too. Also, libraries, churches, doctors' surgeries, schools, gyms, leisure centres etc all often advertise and run mum (and dad) baby groups and coffee mornings, so it's well worth having a look around your local area to see what's on offer, and there are umpteen Facebook groups, too.

LIKE ATTRACTS like so have a think about the type of new parents you might have things in common with – ie culture, hobbies, location – and seek the places and people that interest you.

THE MAIN thing is, DO get out and join something, no matter how small... it really helps in easing any anxiety or blues, and evokes a sense of accomplishment, I promise.

Ten months on from giving birth, I am happy to eat my words and any apprehension I had at leaping into the mum mates' no-man's-land has been pretty much unfounded. On non-work days, I really do enjoy meeting up with the mums, dads and babies for a gossip, moan, sleep-deprivation empathy, and most importantly a good laugh!

'I signed up to NCT classes where you get to mix with other pregnant mums-to-be, experiencing the same fears and emotions. You see, you are not alone. I kept reminding myself that thousands of women give birth every day and then go back for baby number two, so it can't be that bad? Surely? Looking back now, I recognise that my fears were of the unknown.'

Jenni Falconer – TV presenter and mum to Ella

So, keen to meet some parent pals, halfway through my pregnancy, unsure of what to expect, I signed up for NCT antenatal classes, as that seemed like a good start, and something a lot of people seemed to do. Four weeks before our EDD (the estimated due date that all expectant parents become completely obsessed with) my husband (who was dragged) and I rocked up to the local town hall to embark on the course.

Turning up late (of course we did), I don't think we did ourselves any favours in discreetly fitting in – the hubby had come straight from work as a personal trainer and was in sweaty gym gear, and I was caked in glittery telly make-up with a full-on glamour hairdo, fresh from appearing on *Big Brother's Bit on the Side* show – compared to the respectably dressed and well turned-out other parents-to-be.

If you've never had the joy of antenatal, or parentcraft, classes it's worth just signing up to one for a laugh so you can fully appreciate what it entails. It doesn't have to be NCT, which you have to pay for (costs vary depending on location and the type of course), the NHS offer a free one if you prefer (these do tend to get booked up quickly), and there are other options such as hypnobirthing, and private and online antenatal sessions if you prefer to go down a more individual one-to-one route.

However, like so many others, we chose NCT classes. They are extremely popular, and a great way to meet other soon-to-be-parents from your local area. Ours consisted of a dozen or so expectant parents sitting around in a circle, all looking equally as awkward as their neighbouring stranger, clutching cups of tea in those bogey-green cups and saucers from the 1970s that all village halls seem to have, as we were encouraged to share our innermost private thoughts on breasts, vaginas and bodily fluids. It's just so phenomenally surreal, and the genius of it all is that you tend to instantly bond and stick to each other for dear life in mutual fear, horror and hysterical-with-laughter empathy (and awkwardness).

'The Children's Centre activities, baby sensory, swimming etc have been an amazing way of meeting new people in the same boat. I have made a lovely group of friends through various classes. I'm not a very outgoing person but I made myself go to classes and meet up with new people otherwise I would have just been at home going crazy with cabin fever.'

Bronwen – mum to Georgia

My NCT group, many of whom have kindly contributed their experiences to this book, are without a shadow of a doubt the most fabulously witty and empathetic bunch of new mum friends I could ever have wished for. Along with the other lovely mum pals I've picked up along the way through meeting in the labour ward, pregnancy yoga, baby swimming, baby sensory, baby Italian club... (you get the idea), I genuinely never thought I would welcome another bunch of friends into my life so easily and readily. And in those early days of newborn night feeding and post-birth healing, I would have been completely lost without the WhatsApp groups that merrily pinged away every hour of the day (and night) serving as reassurance, empathy and contact with others going through exactly the same thing, at exactly the same time.

None us of knew each other prior to pregnancy and giving birth (I still struggle to remember their surnames now) yet I can list with complete confidence each of their birth stories, babies' habits, and Friday night tipple preferences. I will never forget the refreshing honesty in those early weeks and months that these ladies offered up, a snapshot into their own lives and daily experiences that often mirrored mine, and they helped me feel not quite so alone and incompetent as they offered support, advice (if asked for), and a well-needed giggle at 2am! There are eight girls in my NCT group and there were many times when we were all on the same group message at some ungodly hour with babies attached to our boobs or the bottle, watching the *Jeremy Kyle Show* sign-language version (which denotes how ruddy late it is) and moaning about how '*boring* new babies actually are'.

'I'd be secretly glad when people would message to say they'd had a bad night, as it made me feel not quite so bad.'

Katy – mum to Charlie

I realised that the anxiety I had about making new friends was unfounded. No one wants to be judged or not liked, we are ALL children at heart and fear rejection, but I'm so fortunate that meeting fellow mums has not only been an extremely positive experience for me, but it's also been the absolute icing on the cake in helping me adjust to becoming a mum myself, and I'm very proud and lucky to call these ladies (with their gorgeous babies) my friends too.

'The group has been a huge source of sympathy, encouragement and helpful advice. It's not at all cliquey and probably one of the most positive experiences of female friendship I've ever had. Being able to raise worries and concerns and be listened to by non-judgemental women who "have your back" as it were has been such a massive source of support.'

Sarah – mum to James, aged 12 months

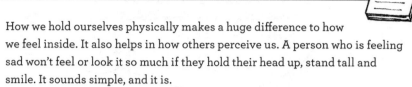

Fake it til you make it

How we hold ourselves physically makes a huge difference to how we feel inside. It also helps in how others perceive us. A person who is feeling sad won't feel or look it so much if they hold their head up, stand tall and smile. It sounds simple, and it is.

Making new friends can be nerve-wracking for anyone and it's important to remember you won't be alone in feeling anxious or nervous at new baby clubs or coffee hang outs. The key is to *look* confident, even if you're not quite feeling it, to help get you out of the house and socialising with other parents – you might be surprised at how much it helps.

Take a deep breath and as you slowly breathe out feel the calmness wash over you.

Stand up nice and tall, shoulders back, head up and walk into whatever room or gathering you might be joining with confidence (even if it feels a bit faked, you'll look like you want to be there).

Hold eye contact with others. It can be hard to do when feeling nervous, but pick out one or two people you like the look of and be sure to talk while looking them in the eye – it gives off warmth and sincerity.

Smile! You might not be feeling particularly chirpy, and you'll have slept less than you've ever done in your life, but mustering up the best smile you can will help you feel better, and others also will naturally warm to you more than if you were down in the dumps. A smile is infectious – try it out.

Keep both feet planted on the floor (if appropriate) – it helps you to stop fidgeting with nerves and unease.

Ask a question. Remember, there's every chance that other new parents have and are going through similar experiences to you, so break the ice and ask a question such as 'how old is your little one?' or simply saying 'hello', or 'what's your baby's name?'

Put your phone away for a bit. A smart phone is most parent's lifeline (I know), but when you're out meeting people, enjoy the fact you have face-to-face company and conversation. Hiding behind a phone can make you seem disinterested and unapproachable.

Getting out and about

What a lot of parents don't fess up to is how damn scary it is to venture outside of the safe confines of your home with a newborn. For lots of us leaving the house with the ticking time bomb of an unpredictable baby that can go off at any minute can cause some serious anxiety issues. It can feel like such a mission for any parent, whether fledgling or not, and what with the screaming, untimely 'poonami' poo explosions, and leaky nipple wet patches on your top (damn those flimsy breast pads!) – it can be bloody embarrassing!

> *'I found motherhood very lonely at first, as the first one in my group of girlfriends, I felt under pressure to still be "me" and act like it hadn't changed me.'*
>
> **Beth – mum to Jacoby and Carys**

I've always been a traveller, someone who enjoys exploring the world. From the age of 16 (when I cut my teeth in showbiz as part of a girlband – blush, ahh those were the days) I have been fortunate to travel the globe. I've filmed kids' TV shows in the

Australian outback, I've walked through the *favelas* of Brazil, and I've eaten all kinds of interesting things in rural China (pig lung soup anyone?). My mother calls me 'worldly'. I just consider myself damn lucky to have had all these wonderful opportunities, and to have seen some incredible places.

So imagine my horror upon leaving the maternity hospital with my precious new addition and realising I was terrified of getting in the car, let alone the prospect of going back out into the big wide world with a new baby. My anxiety was sky high as we made the journey that every parent remembers – 'taking baby home'. Even the most accomplished of drivers it seems pootle along at 15mph, causing tailbacks, while stressing that you might suddenly have a head-on collision. The precious cargo snoozes, totally oblivious, trussed up in the little white hat/babygro combo. Getting into the car, I remember thinking 'I can't do this!' After the confines of the maternity unit, suddenly everything seemed so big and busy, noisy and bright, and it was surreal that everyone else was just going about their daily business.

After a couple of days of being at home in our new little family unit, my husband suggested we pop out for Saturday brunch. What?! Actually leave my safe haven of home comforts, baby paraphernalia and a toilet on tap for when my pelvic floor had an untimely release? To say I was anxious about going out was an understatement, I can't overstate quite how scared I was just to venture a few miles down the road for an eggs benedict.

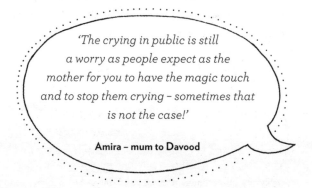

'The crying in public is still a worry as people expect as the mother for you to have the magic touch and to stop them crying – sometimes that is not the case!'

Amira – mum to Davood

A few weeks later still, husband was back at work at this point, I made the brave decision to meet a fellow new mum friend for a coffee. Is there anything more anxiety inducing than driving solo with a newborn strapped in the back? It didn't help that just a few weeks earlier the news had been full of a newborn fatality due to sitting in a car seat for too long, so as I drove at granny speed along the lanes I was anxiously checking my boy in the mirror for signs of distress at every safe moment. I only went two miles to the nearest town, but to my anxious and sleep-deprived self it was such an achievement! I felt nervous, flustered and overwhelmed about where to park, how to get the pushchair out, remembering the baby bag – and of course the baby* – that by the time I arrived at the coffee shop to meet my pal, I was in a bit of a frazzled state.

*I'll fess up here, I once left the baby in the car in the supermarket car park (only for a minute or so thankfully). I'd just totally forgotten for a moment that I was no longer solo in my day-to-day activities – a guilt-ridden, gut-wrenching act that I know I'm far from alone in committing!

Thankfully I soon calmed down and, armed with a much-needed cup of coffee and helped by a friendly face, I soon relaxed a bit and allowed myself to enjoy some grown-up human company for an hour or so. What I didn't realise at the time was that my new friend was equally as nervous as me about being 'out'. I'll never forget getting back home that day and being so proud of myself for managing to accomplish a seemingly small thing for most, but a huge one for me – and her.

Gradually, over time, I experimented with driving a bit further afield, sometimes to a baby massage class at the local council-run Children's Centre, or the weigh-in clinic, and each time I ventured out, I just got that little bit more confident. Having a baby really can take you back to square one in so many ways, it's like learning how to ride a bike from scratch again and having to work out how to peddle, steer and look ahead all at the same time. The feeling of responsibility was a huge challenge.

'Early on, I avoided other mums
as I was worried I wouldn't know the answer to
questions (such as, "how much did your baby
weigh when he was born?") – I felt like people could
see my son didn't have an attachment to me, so to
compensate for this I felt an overwhelming need to tell
everyone I met that he was adopted, as a way of
explaining that I wasn't a terrible mother.'

Erin – adopted mum of Zach

If you're feeling the wobbles about getting out and about with your baby, just remember it's all new, or at least daunting and stressful all over again, so it's completely normal to feel a bit anxious about it. One journey and task at a time, one day at time, don't feel any pressure to do anything you don't feel ready to do, but equally see if you can push yourself just that tiny bit to ensure you're not just stuck at home all the time, especially if you have other children as they'll be keen to get out and about – feeling isolated and lonely isn't going to help that pesky mental health, and let's be honest, being a parent can be really boring too! Maybe you could pop to the supermarket (getting to know how the baby trollies work is another new thing to fathom and master), or head out to the park to meet a friend – anything to help grow your confidence and break up the boredom. You can do it my friend, just go at your pace.

Breaking Point   S.O.S

Breaking up the boredom

Pick one or more of these things to try, and feel free to add any of your own and give them a go. You could either time this for when your baby is down for a nap or you might want to consider getting your partner/a babysitter/friend/mum to give you some time off:

PLAN A PAMPER hour – lock yourself in your bathroom, light a candle, buy a relaxing bath oil (such as lavender), a face pack and a body scrub and just give yourself some time to have a jolly good soak and relax.

PLAN SOMETHING for you. It might be a nail appointment (check out Groupon or Wowcher for local offers), perhaps sitting in a local cafe enjoying some peace and quiet reading a new book, or perhaps having your hair done. Choose something within your budget just for you.

PLAN A COFFEE date – human interaction is so helpful in lifting our mood, even better when it means you have to get out of your house (which can sometimes feel like a baby prison) and physically meet up somewhere. Plan it for a day that suits you and look forward to keeping that date.

TAKE SOME EXERCISE. It might be doing a home exercise DVD or YouTube workout, going for a walk in the local park with a pal, joining a gym, signing up to a yoga class, having a swim and sauna at the local pool. Find something you enjoy – exercise is so important and proven to lift mood and alleviate anxiety.

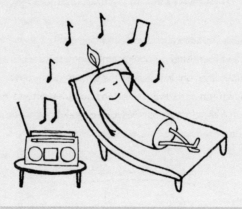

Out with the old

There's no doubt about it, having a baby puts pressure on all the relationships in your life, your partner (if you have one), your family, and your friendships. I'm going to be talking about the changes that occur within a relationship shortly, but for now, I want to shine the spotlight on friendships.

Friendships are like seasons, they come and go, but true friendships stand the test of time whatever the circumstances. However, it's pretty fair to say that friendships can be tested when you chuck a baby into the mix. Now, in an ideal world, your close pals have children around the same time as you so you all evolve from drinking til you puke to changing nappies, together. It never quite works out like this though, and babies can cause cracks and strains in even the most watertight of kinships.

It's a tough course to navigate and many parents feel torn between keeping up with their old lifestyle and friendship groups, or embracing the sofa and take-away for the umpteenth Saturday night in. It takes time to find your groove and work out how to operate as a mum or dad who now can't go out as often as perhaps you once did, and even if you do, that taking a little one along is going to be a whole different experience.

'It was like being back at school again – making new friends and hoping I was part of the cool gang... another point for anxiety. Non-baby friend relationships are now very different. I don't want to be the person who became boring since having a baby but I often feel like I only have that to talk about. I no longer have time for my hobbies or interests because of the baby so I feel like I have nothing interesting to say.'

Cat – mum to Jack, aged two years

We toyed with trying to have it all and attempted to keep up with friends' gatherings and drinks down the pub on a Friday night – and the upshot was it just made me feel crap. A crap friend for not being able to fully commit to a night out, and a crap mum for not just staying in staring at the baby monitor. Day events seemed a good solution. We decided to take our teething six-month-old to a (baby-free) friends' BBQ and spent the majority of the day wheeling him around in the pram, in the garden, in the rain (classic Britain!), to ease his crying, not really speaking to anyone at all and feeling like we had the grumpiest baby in the world ever. In the end we regrettably left having barely eaten a sausage – and of course the minute we did, little man decided to turn off the waterworks and smile adoringly at us for the rest of the evening.

> 'My best mate had a baby
> three months after me. She lives half an hour
> from me yet we barely see each other. It feels so
> strange... surely we should be seeing each other weekly?!
> Her baby is on a strict routine and she is so frightened of
> breaking it that she doesn't try and make plans or want
> to do anything that is further than five minutes away.
> It makes me mad inside.'
>
> **Pia – mum to Mathilda**

Friendships can be tested when you become a parent. You most probably won't be able to respond to messages as quickly, or at all, let alone get round to ringing someone back for a chat as any such spare time may be spent frantically trying to do a wash, cook dinner etc. Like a lot of us, you might also just not give a flying toss and be too exhausted to even have anything to say to anyone anyway, other than reflect on how many feeds your baby is managing, and how much you'd give for a few hours of unbroken sleep. So many mums say they feel so cut off from civilised chat in those first few weeks that they barely know how to, or care about trying to, keep up with the daily news and gossip.

Friends who don't have kids can be tricky to reassure at first as you suddenly disappear off the face of the earth into a baby vortex, and pals who do have kids are dealing with their own issues and adjusting with their own children, and might not have time to invest in friendships of old either.

There's also the awkward and sensitive issue of friends who might be trying for a baby themselves, perhaps they're already pregnant and won't want to hear your moans and groans, some friends may have experienced difficulties such as losing a baby, and others might be going through the undoubtedly stressful experience of having fertility help to conceive, such as IUI or IVF. There are of course also friends who might not be able to have children, yet desperately want them, and some who have actively chosen not to become parents. There are so many circumstances and situations that absolutely might need some very careful handling, but it's important to remember that this doesn't in any way mean you have to feel guilty and pretend all is well, if it's not. Being empathetic, tactful and considerate is important, but it's key not to feel silenced if you need to offload any feelings – perhaps just be sensible in who you confide in.

One new mum-to-be I know feels in a very awkward situation as she's 20 weeks pregnant and feeling awful with sickness and birth anxiety, and yet her friend has tragically just lost her baby at 39 weeks – obviously the most upsetting possible situation, and one that has unfortunately had a big emotional impact on both women and their friendship. Time and space will hopefully enable their friendship to recover, but understandably, the pregnant mum-to-be has taken a back seat to, in her words, 'not flaunt' her growing bump, while her friend grieves. A desperately unjust situation, and a good reminder that there is often a lot of give and take in a friendship.

Generally speaking, empathy for others can really help you to manage any feelings of upset, annoyance or worry regarding a tested friendship. Talk to your friends about any concerns you might have – even a weekly text message can show you they care, and vice versa – and also remember that sometimes people do just move on. There is nothing wrong with that. Ask yourself 'what does this friendship give me?' and the answer can help you decide what you'd like to do going forwards – whichever way, and with whomever you choose.

Cutting loose – the first night OUT out

If you've managed to ease yourself out of the house *with* your baby, eventually, sooner rather than later for some, the time might come for you to venture out of the house *without* your baby. It might be a night with your old mates, an evening with your new mummy mates – whatever the soirée of choice, the first time is undoubtedly one of the most momentous and conversely over-hyped escapes you will make. It's an outing fraught with emotion... nerves, excitement, anxiety, dread, delirium, and will often take a shed load of planning*.

* This last point is especially true if you are breastfeeding as you'll need to work out how the baby can be fed in your absence (whether this is milk you express just before going out, to avoid upsetting your production cycle and leaking everywhere, or formula). What's more, you'll also need to try to get your baby to accept a bottle well in advance of your night out – and this can be more difficult than you might imagine. Once you are out, you really do need to be careful about how much alcohol you drink as it will affect your milk – in all likelihood you'll have to express and throw away the tainted milk you produce while you are out and shortly afterwards, which means you'll need an alternative to give the baby. No wonder mums often can't be bothered and opt to stay in!

Months of abstinence during pregnancy, the early weeks of breastfeeding and general birth recovery has meant you haven't sipped anything other than cordial for yonks, and the prospect of a few glasses of something stronger is, quite frankly, bloody exciting. Added to that, getting out of your vomit-stained tracky bs, popping some actual heels on (steady with this, I fell over straight away having worn nothing but flip-flops for 12 months), and perhaps a smidge of make-up, the first night out after having your baby is a HUGE deal.

So many mums I asked laughed fondly at the memory of their version of 'wetting the baby's head', and you can see why. Us mums can get up to here with the incessant demands of our new babies, angry beyond belief at the constant crying (OMG the ear-splitting CRYING!), and just need a jolly good release with a like-minded crowd. One mum told me that she was once so stressed and fed up with her baby's crying that she stood in her kitchen with the cooker extractor fan on full pelt so it drowned out the screams, while she angrily yelled into a cushion to relieve some of her exasperation! Once her baby finally settled she promptly texted a new mum mate and demanded that a night out was to be planned IMMEDIATELY.

My first night out was pretty much on a par with that of many other mums I speak to. The NCT lot decided on a drink and some food at a local establishment. Turning up at 7pm sharp, the palpable feeling of excitement at a) bagging a babysitter/getting the dad to take a shift b) being out and c) in like-minded company was off the scale. It was almost as if we were under starters' orders as we packed in whatever we could consume in the two-hour window we'd all been afforded by hopefully sleeping babies. Freshers students had nothing on us... the over-excitement versus the fact we hadn't drunk in forever just meant that all the pent-up stress, anxiety, cabin fever and general 'hello again life' just came spilling out of knackered new mums buoyed by the finest sauvignon blanc.

I can't actually remember how the night concluded, but let's just say mums were being picked off one at a time by stressed dads texting frantically, unable to settle fractious four-month-olds, and after a couple of hours I, too, bundled myself into a cab home. I'm not proud of the following scene but much to my husband's annoyance, I arrived home, staggered through the door 'steaming', and spent the next six hours with my head down the loo. My penance was being made to do the 5am feed. OMG worst moment ever.

I wasn't alone in my state... most of the other girls reported similar scenes back at their homes, and the point is this: we NEEDED a night to cut loose. OK, getting drunk accidentally on three drinks isn't the coolest thing I've ever done, but for a new mother, fizzing with stress and desperate to let it out and have some fun, it was just what I needed.

I'm not for one minute suggesting you go out and follow my irresponsible actions (and the hangover was brutal) but the need to have some time off, even for a few hours, is essential for a parent of a young baby. A chance to remember who you are, and an opportunity to regain a bit of the old you. It's also super important to hang out with your other half too, it can be a bit of a mission organising babysitters but it's really worth making the effort to make it happen, after yonks of 'shift eating', having a meal together where you're not rushing, bolting it down in two minutes, can be a relationship game changer! Couple time is key in regrouping and communicating with each other, without your little one interrupting.

'It was our wedding anniversary four weeks after the birth of our son so my parents offered to babysit for a few hours so we could go out for a meal. OMG, it was surreal being out without the baby, we felt giddy with excitement yet nervous about leaving him. After weeks of feeling like crap, it was just nice to be out, together, and wearing decent clothes!'

Meryl – mum of Sonny, aged four months

How to... enjoy your first day or night out

ENLIST the help of someone you trust to care for the baby – your other half, a parent, in-law, friend or highly trained and vetted professional.

IF YOU CAN, make sure you feed your baby just before you leave to give you peace of mind that you have at least a few hours until the next one is due.

IF YOU WANT TO, experiment with expressing breast milk or trying a bottle at least a few days before you're due out so someone else can feed the baby if they need to while you're away.

ARRANGE to go somewhere fairly near home so you can feel reassured you can get back quickly if necessary.

CHOOSE to go out with some like-minded pals – who get how much you need it and any time constraints you might be under.

TAKE IT EASY! Enjoy your few hours of 'you time', but remember to be safe and sensible (ish) ... so you can enjoy the nice after-effects of your time off too.

The heat is on

Let's turn our attention to the 'significant other' in your life, if you have one. The person you hopefully chose to embark on this crazy baby-mummy-and-daddy journey with.

Anyone who says 'let's have a baby, it'll be the most romantic experience ever' needs to have their head flushed down a loo! Having a baby and 'romance' is a pipe dream best saved for the Hollywood movies. In our case, the most romance either of us has seen in the 10 months since Enzo was born is an early night wearing a clean pair of PJs (we genuinely get excited about this). Now, I know plenty of people DO feel smoochy cutesy and overcome with love and lust for their other half the minute they become a parent – and that's lovely, truly – but for us, the moment our little boy joined us, I don't mind admitting, was the moment we were seriously tested as a couple.

In the first few weeks after our son's arrival, we had two of the most almighty rows ever. And I mean those real screamy, shouty, slightly foaming at the mouth, ones. The cause? Who bloody knows eh? ... but lack of sleep, feeling overwhelmed, insecurity, anxiety and hormones didn't help. Having never endured successive broken nights of sleep in our lives, the competitive tiredness between us was almost worthy of an Oscar. *Obviously* I won each time as we growled and grunted at each other, I blatantly (and probably unfairly) pulled the 'I've JUST given birth out of my VAGINA' card every time, which kind of made most of his mutterings null and void. Looking back now, we can have a good laugh (almost) and reminisce about the 'dark days' when all we wanted to do was stab each other in the eye, and curse the other for getting more sleep. It was pathetic how we'd try and score points with the 'well YOU got 15 minutes more than me last week...'-type arguments.

Based on research carried out by the Relationship Research Institute in Seattle, USA, parenting advice mecca *Babble* reports that almost one in six relationships break up after the birth of a baby. My belief is that if we understand and accept *why* relationships feel so tested at this time in life, and do something to keep things on an even keel, more people will be able to salvage their love and keep the flame alive until easier times arrive – for they almost certainly will.

'We set up two camps... one in the bedroom, and one in the sitting room. We'd take turns to get up for feeds and bed swap – baby feeding took place on the sofa surrounded by pillows, rugs and DVD boxsets, the off-duty parent got to go back to sleep in the actual bed. Essential survival yes, romantic it was not.'

Robin – surrogate dad to Lily, aged 18 months

Relationships take a heck of a shake when a baby joins as the third wheel. Suddenly there is a permanent distraction, and this is only exacerbated by having further children. We run the risk of showering all our love on to the baby, with little left for the other half, especially if other children are jealous and being very demanding of what love and attention we have to spare. A baby needs so much attention, love and care that it really can be all too much to even consider sharing your affection. And I was that person – I didn't feel I had enough love for even my son initially, let alone my husband! Parents can feel rejected or sidelined by their other half, now that a gurgling baby takes the lion's share of cuddles. Add in a knackered, recovering mum, a stressed dad, a baby who feeds on demand every few hours, chores needing doing, potential post-birth body hang ups, and of course, the dreaded discussion of... S – E – X...

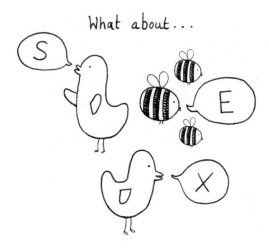

The very activity that got every parent in this situation in the first place, post birth this can become a major elephant in the room, the one act that, let's face it, neither side particularly wants to do.

I'm going to be delving more into post-birth sex anxiety, and the different perspectives from men and women, in later chapters.

We need to remember who we have chosen to join us on this adventure, and allow them to grow and adapt with us. Change doesn't happen overnight (although the baby's arrival probably did!), so give things time to settle as you all adjust, and keep bickering to a minimum by trying to notice the nicer things, not the irritating ones.

> 'I actually hated my
> husband... I'd gone from loving him
> more than anything, to seething with
> resentment as he slept soundly next to me as I
> grappled with nipple cream and a hungry baby.
> How dare he get more sleep than me!'
>
> **Sandi – mum to Thomas, aged six months**

Notice the nice stuff

In those moments of all-consuming baby tyranny, it can be tricky to focus on the other important people in your life. Tiredness, soreness, worry, anxiety, stress... can all affect a relationship, so catch yourself before you feel resentment or negativity and try to remind yourself of your partner's good points. It'll do wonders for your bonding, but also ease any tension between you.

Have a think about your partner and what qualities, acts of kindness or support you are grateful for. This is an example of my list, so just a template, but do make up your own:

He makes me endless cups of tea.

When I see him smile at the baby it makes my heart melt.

He runs me a bath without me having to ask, makes me eat when I forget, and remembers to feed the cat.

I get a big cuddle and kiss when I need it the most.

I get told I look beautiful even though I don't feel it at the moment.

He sometimes agrees to do a full night of feeds so I can catch up on sleep.

I love it when we go for a family walk – just the three of us.

Devise your own lists, and keep reminding each other what you like most about the other. Let the appreciation outweigh the criticism. Happy couple, happy baby.

Dr Reetta says...

Getting used to the new you
We all know that relationships are central to our functioning, well-being and moods. We also know that a new baby will lead to changes in all our relationships. What we often don't realise is how the transition to parenthood impacts on these – for many parents it can be quite unexpected.

But it makes sense – there's so much changing – whether it's our shifting identities (you might wonder whether you'll ever be 'you' again), new roles and how they are divided (and can cause conflict if there's a lack of understanding of each other's lives if one is at work and the other at home). Add to that an often new burden of financial responsibility if one of you is on maternity or paternity leave. Over time your new identity will develop and adapt to absorb your new parenting role, but there will be bits of your old identities that you might miss – in you or in your partner. Try to be patient – most parents will manage to find *some* time for their relationships once they settle into parenthood.

If you have a partner, you should anticipate and allow for changes in your relationship. The transition to parenthood can be stressful, even in a very well-functioning relationship, and there may be feelings of frustration and rejection. Expect the first year to be tough, as you are each finding your place in the family, negotiating a balance between family time and individual time. Having a baby can bring up difficult feelings from your own childhood or about your own family relationships – perhaps you don't have a close bond with your parents, or they have died – becoming a parent can really bring feelings of sadness about these to the fore. You will each have had your own different experiences of being parented that you will bring to parenting your baby together. It may be that you want to be very different to your parents, or pick aspects of their parenting that you like and not adopt ones that you don't like. Similarly, your partner will bring their experiences and views.

Anna describes a lovely-sounding group of friends, old and new, in her life. Making and keeping friends isn't easy for everyone, however. I wonder whether it is Anna's honesty and openness to talking about difficult aspects of life that have enabled all these friendships to flourish?

Tops tips for dealing with friendships and relationships

1. If you have a partner, keep communicating and working together as much as possible. Have realistic expectations of each other and regularly schedule in some time together. Accept that most of the time there isn't a quick or easy solution to anything that is to do with relationships. Talk together about your thoughts about parenting and where they come from – could that help to explain why an aspect of being a parent is tricky for you or your partner?

If you are worried about your relationship or feel you might be on the verge of separating, have a look at www.relate.org.uk and their 'new parents' section. You can also try a free online chat with a Relate counsellor through their website. Speak to your health visitor or GP to find out about local support for parents, including couples' counselling.

2. Changing how you behave towards other people is often the easiest way to change how they relate to you. What are your personal triggers for feeling frustrated or upset with people? For new parents, such as Anna and her husband, a common trigger is sleep deprivation. When you're tired, it is difficult to regulate your emotions. Are there unhelpful patterns that seem to keep repeating with friends or partners? Do you need to develop new ways of coping with these situations?

3. How would you like to come across when you meet and get to know other parents and potential friends? Anna's Activity Alert 'Fake it til you make it' is a great place to get some ideas for those interactions. Facing your fears, gradually, is a useful principle to keep in mind if you are feeling anxious about the social aspects of parenthood. You will learn that those situations tend to get easier the more you expose yourself to them. Any negative self-talk you notice, replace it with something more helpful and balanced.

Tackling negative self-talk

This is important because negative self-talk can make you feel bad and behave in self-defeating ways. Firstly, you need to become aware and start spotting your negative self-talk. Secondly, you need to challenge those thoughts and look at alternative ways to view the situation. What is the evidence for and against what you are thinking? Is this a thought or a fact? What alternative perspectives are there: what would you think about this situation if you were having a good day or were feeling more confident, what would you say to a friend with this thought? Is thinking this way fair or helpful to you? The ultimate goal is to speak to yourself as you would to someone you care for, by being fair, kind and not expecting perfection.

Breaking unhelpful patterns in behaviour

What are your unhelpful patterns in behaviour that keep repeating in your relationships with family and friends? It may be around pleasing people, not being able to say 'no', not being able to be yourself or feeling you have failed when something goes less than perfectly. It's important to think of unhelpful behaviours as these are linked to feelings, including anxiety. Becoming aware and acknowledging patterns in behaviour is key to addressing them. What alternative ways of behaving can you think of or have you observed in other people? Think of small ways of altering your behaviour and experiment how the changes in behaviour influence how you feel.

7
GOING BACK TO WORK (OR NOT)

The 'circus juggler' feeling

There is no such thing as a perfect parent, so just be a real one.

Sue Atkins, parenting expert

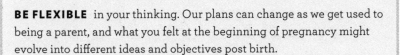

Baby steps...

BE FLEXIBLE in your thinking. Our plans can change as we get used to being a parent, and what you felt at the beginning of pregnancy might evolve into different ideas and objectives post birth.

DISCUSS your thoughts, concerns and feelings about whether you'd like to return to work, or not, with your partner or close friend or family member – it can be helpful to gain some extra perspective and reassurance.

ULTIMATELY do what's best for you and your baby and go with your instinct. Nothing has to stay as it is forever, but it's important to take any unnecessary pressure and anxiety off you and do what is best for *your* family.

Bankrolling baby

While conducting my own research into which areas of parenting cause the most anxiety for parents, without a doubt, the 'are you going back to work?' dilemma is one of the most emotive, quickly followed by the 'do you want or *have* to go back to work?' loaded question.

As a freelancer I always knew that the moment I got pregnant, I wasn't going to be eligible for Statutory Maternity Pay or any maternity packages. It's something I've never moaned about and have always accepted that it's my choice to be my own boss, so, as are a lot of things in life, it's swings and roundabouts. Yes, I get to choose when I go on holiday, and I don't need permission to have a day off, but I'm on my own when it comes to getting any extra financial support when starting a family.

Lots of us benefit from either generous company maternity packages, or the government employee benefit of SMP (Statutory Maternity Pay). For those who are self-employed or unable to qualify for SMP, it's Maternity Allowance (MA). If you're an adoptive or surrogate parent, you may be eligible for Statutory Adoption Pay or Leave, which depending on your type of employment, carries the same 'rules' with time off and amounts received, as SMP and MA. Whatever your situation, it's worth exploring at the very least to see what you might be entitled to, and although not squillions of pounds, it can serve as a much-needed income source during the first few months, and up to the best part of the first year.

Dads, or partners, also qualify for paid parental leave, with the old rule of 'two weeks' paternity leave' now including an additional six months if the mother goes back to work within the first year. Basically, in the UK parenting can be juggled much more fairly, there are options and this can only be a good thing.

For me, other than the good old family allowance state benefit of £20 a week, the options were pretty much nil (as I own my own business I didn't qualify for MA), but that was something I'd already made peace with long before we started trying for a baby, (I guess you can't miss something you've never had), and my (also self-employed) hubby and I made sure we squirrelled away some savings to serve as a safety net for when the baby was born. Thankfully we've both always been OK at handling our finances. I think being a sole trader really does teach you to save for a rainy day (or when Mr Tax Man decides to come a'knocking) so we were fairly prepared when our little man came to join our family – but by no means were we well off and able to sit by being full-time parents for the next couple of years.

I appreciate that we are not the norm, and most new parents are faced with the task of telling their boss that they're going to be going on maternity leave, something that most find more than a little nerve-wracking.

'I work in a male-dominated
company and I was so worried about
everyone finding out that I was pregnant,
I didn't want to let my team down and I feared
I would be judged for needing to take a year off to
have my baby. My boss was really good about
it fortunately and has been supportive.'

Zara – mum to Cora, aged 12 months

And once little one is here, there are just so many mixed feelings about work. Do I *want* to go back? Do I *have* to go back? *Can* I go back? Some of us can't stand the thought of going back to our jobs, some of us have to resume our employment sooner than others for financial reasons, and some of us really want to get back into the work groove. All the mums I speak to have an opinion on the 'going back to work or not' dilemma, with so many feeling genuine anxiety and stress at the very thought – including the ones who want to go back ASAP. Will my boss be understanding? What if I need time off if the baby gets ill? Can I get part-time hours or adjust my hours to suit childcare? Will I even be earning anything at all once childcare and travel is taken into account? So many questions and we all just pray that our place of work will be empathetic to our needs and requests.

'I knew I had to go back
[to work] after six months to help pay the
bills but I felt so anxious speaking to my work
about how that might pan out. I desperately needed
to be able to leave at 5.30pm to pick my son up from
nursery by 6pm. At 5.59pm I'd get him but every
day feels like a mission to ensure I leave on time.'

Natasha – mum to Bertie, aged seven months

Now with all this in mind, what I didn't personally anticipate was how much I would miss work the moment I became a mother, and above anything else, this caused me the greatest feelings of guilt and anxiety – and surprise.

I have always been the maternal type, I love children – I entertained millions as a kids' TV presenter for several years – and am definitely a Mother Hen. I always thought that the moment I became a mum would be the moment work would take a back seat, be no longer important to me. And this is the point about parenting thoughts and feelings – we often have no control over them and how they will manifest when actually put to the test.

I *did* miss my old life, and the anxiety and shock of the whole birthing experience was making me crave normality. Working in therapy and being on TV and radio, and mixing in the world of entertainment is *my* normal. Prior to being a mum it was all I'd done for 18 years and this new mum role was so alien to me – I just yearned for the familiarity and comfort of 'the old me', and that meant being able to work. What has interested, and comforted, me is that I know I'm not alone in this feeling.

> 'As a previous career woman,
> I felt the need to go back to work quite
> soon after the birth of my first baby. I did not feel
> guilty for it and did not feel judged by too many
> people. My position was something I had earned
> and I didn't want to give it all up because I was
> also now a mum.'
>
> **Liz – mum of two**

Grieving for the old you

Feeling like I was losing a grip on the old me was a big source of my post-natal anxiety. I'm so lucky that I have always loved and thrived on work. I consider myself never to have really done a day's work in my life, as I enjoy it, and I love the variety of my job working in therapy, media and broadcasting. No week is ever the same and I thrive on the unpredictability. It's always kept me on my toes and without this buzz, I suddenly felt very stripped bare. It's completely bonkers to think of it now (particularly as I'm beavering away in work mode on this book) but I feared suddenly letting 18 years of hard graft go. I was terrified that now I had a baby no one would employ me again, writing me off as a 'mum' and therefore no longer available, or worse still, desirable.

Looking back, losing one role overnight (being me), and gaining a new one (being mummy) straight away was a massive shock. There was no transition or settling-in period, and the sudden job swap from working woman to mum was mega. I had gone from conducting a work conference call the day before I went into labour to mum mode. I put way too much pressure on myself from the off, and if I could give myself back then any advice now it would be to trust in change and allow it to settle down. Almost a year on I'm still learning how to juggle things but it's becoming clearer each day, and as the anxiety has settled, so have my priorities – with my son above anything taking top spot.

Change can be scary so it's important to process the change that becoming a new parent brings – in fact it's healthy and important to deal with any feelings about the loss of your old life. Nothing marks the end of our carefree years more than suddenly having a little dependant in tow, and you may find yourself wistfully thinking back to when you could dash out without having to pack up half of Mothercare into your car first, or agree to Friday night drinks at the drop of a hat.

Grieving is a healthy part of accepting and coping with change, so put all feelings of guilt and regret to one side, allow any feelings of loss to just 'be' and remind yourself that just because you may miss the old you it doesn't mean that that person isn't there (she totally is) and it also doesn't make you a lesser parent. Being honest about your feelings is hugely cathartic, be reassured that the old you is still very much present alongside the new – in fact let's bring the two of you together.

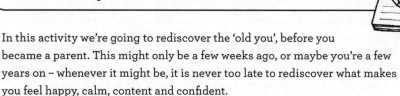

Memory moments

In this activity we're going to rediscover the 'old you', before you became a parent. This might only be a few weeks ago, or maybe you're a few years on – whenever it might be, it is never too late to rediscover what makes you feel happy, calm, content and confident.

We're going to use our senses and imagination to explore who you are and bring all positive feelings, thoughts and experiences into the here and now.

Take a few moments now to sit or lie quietly. Do it wherever you can – the sofa, the loo, bed, bath, or even the car while baby is having a nap – if possible (not in the car!), close your eyes as this will help you to focus.

Cast your mind back to before you had children... Choose a scenario to help really visualise yourself... perhaps you're at work, or on holiday with mates... Allow your mind to settle on an 'image' of yourself – it might be a moving image like a movie, or a still one like a photograph.

With this image firmly in your mind, I want you to explore this 'you' even further. What do you see? What makes you happy? Perhaps it's having a good gossip with a friend. What do you like to do to relax? Maybe it's watching a movie? What makes you feel confident? Perhaps a colleague praising your work? Have a good think about what the old you is like and what helps you to feel a familiar sense of calm and purpose.

Engage your senses even more and explore anything that helps you to feel even more comforted, perhaps a familiar sound (for example, I like the sound of a busy coffee shop as it reminds me of positive work meetings and meeting pals), or a smell (ditto the smell of fresh coffee), or even a taste.

By recalling all these positive memories, we are reminding ourselves of who we *are*, what makes us feel comforted, positive and safe, and therefore calming down any feelings of insecurity and anxiety – the old you is still very much part of the new you... you've just reminded yourself.

Any time you feel a bit unsure about who you are, or any feelings of missing your life before baby, allow yourself to remember all the things you thought, felt and did before you became a parent. And why not even go one step further and introduce one or two activities back into your life – such as getting your nails done, having a gossip with a friend, enjoying a Friday curry night, relaxing with a coffee and magazine, using the gym crèche and enjoying a swim or exercise class – just to remind yourself that you are very much still you.

Bringing the old and new parts of our life together can help the transition into parenthood feel much less daunting.

To work or not to work...? That is the question

Once I started to get my anxiety and general 'I'm not sure who I am' feeling back under control a bit, I sat down with my husband and had a frank chat about what I wanted, and needed, outside of my mum role. The social life thing didn't really bother me, certainly not at first. I've always been a home bird and not a lover of all-nighters (I'm rubbish at staying up late and drinking), much preferring to cuddle up in bed with the baby. It was the career aspect that caused the biggest inner conflict. Having said that I have mum mates who couldn't have been more opposite to me, couldn't have given a flying toss about work initially, and instead craved the opportunity just to escape to the local pub on a Friday night to catch up with friends, and engage in some normal non-baby chat for a few hours. As one eloquently put it, 'meh, work shmerk'.

I had decided to go with the flow with work and just see how it went, but I didn't anticipate doing much for a good few months or so after giving birth, assuming I'd just not want to. I'd been hosting a Saturday night radio show that had to go on hold – I tried to go back after six weeks but the late night of work with the sleep deprivation just wasn't conducive to keeping myself healthy and well – so I made the decision to take an extended break. A regular 'job' I realised, even if for just one evening a week, just wasn't going to be sustainable so soon into becoming a mum, particularly one battling post-natal anxiety. But I also acknowledged that I needed to do something work wise in order to keep me feeling like me.

'I went back to work really early – my daughter was not quite five months. I cried every day for a fortnight when I dropped her off, but I knew this was the best thing for us both, the way my brain was wired meant I would be a far better mother if I had something else to think about and keep me busy alongside all my new duties,'

Grania – mum to Billy, aged six months

The guilt I felt at not being entirely fulfilled by motherhood at first was huge. I was so aware of other friends trying to conceive, who would give their eye teeth to have what I had – and don't get me wrong, I was unbelievably grateful for my healthy beautiful baby – yet I knew that in order for me to feel truly content I somehow needed to keep my hand in with work. I love my son but I KNOW that I'm not alone in thinking and feeling this.

After a heart-to-heart with my husband, and a good few tears, we decided that I would do the odd job here and there in order to help me feel less anxious about 'losing' my career woman status. I had a hunch this would boost my self-esteem and confidence, give me some 'me time' and allow me to resume my role as mummy with full appreciation – and thank goodness, it worked. From a couple of months into motherhood onwards, I accepted the occasional freelance job hosting events, or making a TV appearance, or a one-off therapy session, and the combination of working mum, even early on, really did help in alleviating my new-mum cabin fever and anxiety. I was able to tap into the old me, which helped me accept and enjoy the new me.

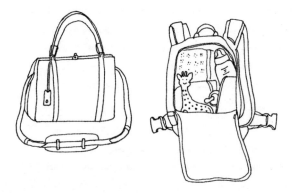

It's often the simple things in life that bring the most pleasure, and nothing is more true than a few hours of being me, not 'just mum'. Leaving the house for a few hours with my 'work hat' on, carrying an actual handbag (instead of my usual bulging baby changing bag), a slick of make-up and enjoying a hot take-away coffee, would, and does, honestly make me feel like a million dollars. Those few hours where I'm being 'career Anna' and earning the pennies for my family to boot, does more for my self-esteem, self-confidence and mental well-being than anything.

> *'I really miss work and want to go back, but am also terrified as I'll have been off for nearly a year, and fear I'll have forgotten how to do things.'*
>
> **Katya – mum to Lena, aged seven months**

I'm not saying this route is for everyone – in fact I'm most probably in the minority by choosing to work after only a few months of entering motherhood, but I also know that I am not alone in this. Becoming a parent is so bespoke that no one can really know how they are going to feel. I know plenty of career mums who have sworn they'd be back at work within weeks of giving birth, but then loved parenthood so much they've never gone back, and then others who thought they'd never want to work again the moment they had a baby, and yet find themselves cutting their maternity leave short in order to get back to their job. You just can't tell which way you'll go, and how you'll feel until you're in the moment – and that's OK.

> *'Twelve months ago I was telling everyone "of course I'm coming back to work, I don't want to just be a mum and give up on all I've worked hard to achieve"; and now, having been back a week, all I'm thinking is "oh f**k, I don't want to work anymore, I no longer care about my job and feel totally out of my depth."'*
>
> **Cathy – mum to Chaz, aged 12 months**

When work isn't an option

It's the dream isn't it to be able to choose whether we work or not, but realistically the majority of us don't get the choice... most of us simply HAVE to return to work after we've taken some sort of maternity leave. A recent National Childbirth Trust (NCT) study found that 80 per cent of all new mums go back to work, with three in four saying that household finances was their main reason for returning. Quality and cost of childcare is a key influence, particularly for working mothers, with the other most important factors cited as keeping up to date with professions, and enjoyment in work. Single mothers are less likely to return to employment (63 per cent) than women who are in relationships (82 per cent), largely due to childcare costs and little financial incentive to return. Only one in ten women plan to stay at home with their child on a full-time basis.

Deciding not to go back to work and instead choosing to stay at home and rear your children, I believe, is without a doubt one of the most admirable jobs in the world! One worthy of a snazzy award or something, for stay-at-home parents are made of strong stuff. The days I am at home caring for my son are some of the most rewarding yet exhausting days ever. I generally look like I feel – knackered. Going to work on the odd day each week is a genuine holiday in comparison, one where I get to eat actual meals and drink hot beverages.

'The reality is that after a while, the pressures of nursery drop-off, the commute, working in a fast-paced environment, running a team and house did lead to stress and anxiety. It's sad for me to know that there are many other women (primarily) that face this pressure every day – it's impossible to have it all and I am left resentful and frustrated that more is not done today to support women going back to work.'

Lucy – mum of three

Often the reasons behind becoming a stay-at-home parent are financial. It's most often not a choice, but instead the sensible decision when weighing up childcare costs versus your salary – most parents report they're barely breaking even once the childcare costs have eaten up the majority of the monthly pay cheque. And when you factor in the cost of the daily commute, in a lot of cases it simply doesn't make financial sense to return to work.

'I've just got my first pay cheque for my new reduced working hours. After nursery fees I really don't know why I'm bothering. I keep telling myself it's worth it to keep my job open, pension going, brain ticking over, but it seems a lot of hard work and disruption to our lives for such a small amount each month. Oh well...'

Claire – mum to Jody, aged 13 months

Then there's the negotiating how much you work. Some women happily return to work full time, others are keen to explore a job-share scheme, and a lot of working mums ask their employers for part-time or flexible working hours in order to fit in with their childcare drop-off/pick-up times, and to help find a work/home balance each week.

One mum pal told me how much she loved her job but she had no choice but to hand in her notice once her year's maternity leave was up as her employer just couldn't offer her anything other than five days a week back – basically her old job, which is the legal obligation, but they wouldn't budge on giving her part-time working hours. This situation has left her wondering 'what do I do now?' Like so many of us, she loved her job, was really proud of her role working in a busy team, and was devastated about giving it up. Her reasoning, when she weighed it all up, was that five days a week of childcare costs and not seeing her daughter as much as she would like just wasn't worth the emotional or financial strain.

'I must say I've found it hard to stomach all the corporate bullshit. When you've been out of it for a year it's hard not to say, "it doesn't matter!"'

Federica – mum to Luna, aged 12 months

It's a scenario I hear over and over again, mums wanting/needing to return to their place of work, but trying to juggle the new role of motherhood with the job of old takes some serious working out – and an empathetic boss.

There are rules and employment laws in place to protect working parents. If your workplace has an HR department, they will be the team to get in touch with to help with your transition back. It might be that you deal with your boss directly and if so, it's always worth being clued up on your rights before you go in for any working hours' negotiation. The Citizens Advice Bureau (CAB) can offer all the advice and maternity employment guidelines you might need. Staying or Keeping in Touch (KIT) days are part of a 'Phased Return to Work' policy, which are paid days, and a great idea to ease yourself back in and familiarise yourself with everyone, the building, job requirement etc.

'I always thought that I'd want to go back to work by around nine months, but when I got to the six-month mark he still felt so young for me to return to work. I've also found that my view on my career has changed and that I'd actually like to go in a different direction.'

Hannah – mum to George, aged 11 months

It's also very important to communicate with your employers and be clear about what you'd like and how it can serve you *both* best. You may have initially agreed to go back to your pre-baby full-time position, which legally has to be kept open to you, but you are entitled to ask for a change in hours and job role, although a boss doesn't necessarily have to agree to giving you what you want – it has to work for everyone. Whatever you decide, hopefully amicably, don't be afraid to enforce the parameters you are going back to work within. If you've agreed to start and finish at a certain time then be strict about sticking to it, if your baby is suddenly ill and the childcare needs you to pick him/her up, then make sure you've addressed this hypothetical situation when you start back so you don't feel any guilt or stress, and think ahead to any potential clash situations that might be avoided with careful time planning and communication, eg your toddler's jabs, or other routine health-check appointments.

'I have a new hatred of everyone I work with (no one else has children) all saying how tired they are all the time. They don't know the meaning of the word!'

Claudia – mum to Maya, aged 12 months

It's also good to communicate your working schedule to your colleagues so you feel in control of any less-than-supportive attitudes. Working late isn't an option any more, with a baby needing picking up from childcare, so hours mainly need to be negotiated and stuck to rigidly. All it takes is one tut from a non-parent colleague as you log off your computer bang on 5pm to make you feel rubbish. Workmates without kids in the main just don't get the sheer exhaustion of being up several times in the night with a teething toddler, so sympathy might be minimal as you rub the invisible grit of sleep deprivation out of your eyeballs during the morning meeting. If you're still breastfeeding the stress and anxiety overload of ensuring your breast pads are correctly stuck in your bra as you conduct a team talk, and the faff of expressing full-to-bursting boobs in the staff toilet is yet another thing to factor in to your day.

Breaking Point   S.O.S

TALK TO your boss. If you're feeling in any way stressed, anxious or out of your depth with your job role, don't suffer in silence. If your boss isn't approachable, have a think about your next port of call and ask to speak to them in confidence.

IT'S NOT a weakness to admit that you're struggling or need more help to readjust to a working parent life. Colleagues aren't mind readers and instead of plodding along feeling miserable, see what changes can be made to ease the pressure off.

KNOW WHEN enough is enough. Sometimes we realise that what we hoped we could do, isn't in fact in our best interests. If you're feeling like you can't cope and that even with changes and communication, the role isn't working for you, that's OK. It takes great strength and self-awareness to weigh up the pros and cons and make the right decision for you and your family.

> *'I think my mental health has been worse since going back to work. I'm more anxious and feel stressed about numerous things including work things that wouldn't have bothered me previously. Does my son get enough of me? I enjoy my job but wish I could be at home full time to make the most of him.'*
>
> **Catherine – mum to Dillon, aged two years**

So my conclusion is this: being a parent is one heck of a juggling act, and yes, you become a master at doing a zillion things all at once, but it's also important to check in with yourself every few months to assess how you're feeling about your current work set up, how much money you're earning, how much you *need* to earn, and whether you can, want or need to make any changes. It takes bravery to be self aware and notice what is, and isn't working.

Be realistic about what you can and can't afford, having kids doesn't *have* to cost an arm and a leg, but it's certainly a financial pressure to shoulder. Be kind to yourself and weigh up decisions that have a financial burden, for example, do you *need* a swanky new family wagon or will a smaller secondhand car be just as adequate (and cheaper), and perhaps leave that expensive loft extension until things are less manic if it means you'd end up working to the point of a breakdown in order to pay for it. If you're thinking about adding to your family at some point, you might also feel the longer term benefit of planning your finances and employment options in advance, before you crack on with another child – it can just take the pressure off any unexpected financial surprises.

Whether you work full time, part time, freelance, don't work, stay at home, use childcare, co-parent... Whatever your set-up and choices, every parent is a professional at spinning plates – fact! We all have good days, off days... days when we feel like a spinning top, but as the quote says at the beginning of this chapter, there is no such thing as a perfect parent, so just be a real one.

How to... go back to work

WHEN YOU first ask for maternity leave your employer will give you a date to return to work. The assumption will be a year unless you tell them you'd like to return sooner.

IF YOU'D LIKE to change your work start date, tell your employer when you'd like to start back and give them at least eight weeks' notice.

IF YOU DECIDE not to return to work, your contract will tell you what notice to give. If you have no contract, you need to give at least one weeks' notice. You should check if you are owed any holiday pay or if you need to pay back any maternity pay.

YOU HAVE a right to return to your work after taking maternity leave, and are entitled to return to the same job if you've been away for 26 weeks or less. Your pay and conditions must be the same, or better, than they would be if you hadn't been away.

IF YOU'VE been on maternity leave for more than 26 weeks it is maternity discrimination if you are not allowed to return to work or are offered a different job without a strong reason.

YOU CAN ask your employer for flexible working at any time. It could mean changing your days or hours, working from home, or switching from shifts to a regular work pattern. Ask if you can have a trial to see if this is doable.

YOUR EMPLOYER doesn't have to agree to flexible working but they should arrange a meeting, give you a decision within three months, and give you their answer in writing, including the reasons if they refuse.

Childcare dilemmas

Do you remember that cartoon character the Road Runner? He used to leg it along a vast desert ravine, dodging 'Acme' dynamite and those comical bombs, often getting flattened along the way by something amusing, and then he would come to a crossroads where he was completely flummoxed about which way to go next. This is very much how it is as a parent – we're often racing along at a rate of knots, blagging it, never quite sure which route to take next, and constantly coming across another set of crossroads. When it comes to going back to work after having a baby, there is no manual that we can follow in order to make sure we're doing it right. We have to give instinct and rational thinking the upper hand here, and take the path that suits our individual needs best.

Timing is a big deal. As we know, some people simply *have* to return to work, mainly for financial or career reasons, and they may have little control over when. Others *want* to resume their working life but have some flexibility to choose when, and some make the decision that work is no longer part of their future as a parent, preferring – or having – to leave, or put on hold, employment. Whatever your decision, timing is often a major factor in the decision-making process. Timing, and pressure.

> *'He was 11 weeks old when I returned to work, but as my mum and dad were my childcare, although at the time it wasn't particularly nice, it was a must and we just did what we needed to do.'*
>
> **Maria – mum to Arthur, aged 13 months**

Assuming going back to work is a very possible reality, the decision-making dilemma about childcare then kicks in. It's a terrifying unchartered territory and it's unfairly loaded with judgement and guilt. My feeling? As long as your little one is being properly cared for, nurtured and essentially happy, then that's a pretty good start isn't it? As much as I knew I needed and wanted to work in small doses fairly soon after my boy's birth, I was also extremely anxious about leaving him with anyone else.

And let's be honest, I was also *very* tetchy about anyone passing judgement about my decision to have Enzo looked after occasionally. I was still dealing with my anxiety issues and nothing ramped up my guilt, paranoia and anxiety more than anyone questioning *why* I was working, and who was looking after my son? I constantly sought advice and reassurance from others in order to be OK with it.

My husband and I are very fortunate to have ace grandparents for our son, our parents are so supportive and helpful – but we equally have never wanted to burden them too much, or take the mickey with childcare. It was my and my husband's decision to have a baby so his welfare and upbringing is our responsibility. The grandparents are great, and help loads, but understandably they either work or have their own commitments so we don't like to call upon them too regularly – it just wouldn't be fair. However, from four months in, work ramped up and we found ourselves needing a little bit of extra help on the odd day one of us couldn't look after the baby ourselves, but we had no idea where to search for it.

Having never even entertained the idea of childcare, and not really knowing what on earth to look for, the answer was closer to home than we thought, as it was actually my trusted community midwife, who had been a rock throughout the pregnancy, who served as the answer to our prayers. Her own kids were now well into their teens but had been looked after when they were younger by a wonderful childminder who just so happened to live a couple of miles from us, and even though she was starting to wind down towards retirement, she was very happy to help us out for a bit. And that is how the lovely Pauline came into our lives.

Enzo was four-and-a-half months old when we first entrusted him to Pauline for a couple of hours. I was wretched with nerves, sick with worry, and as anxious as could be! I didn't want to tell anyone I had 'left' him with someone other than family as I feared being judged so badly. We'd had a couple of stay and play sessions prior to his first solo one, and all our initial fears eased as Pauline, clearly used to dealing with super-anxious new parents, quickly put our minds at rest with her obvious skill, knowledge and gentle nature.

Pauline looked after Enzo every Wednesday for a few hours for several months, until she sadly had to give up childminding altogether due to family reasons, but we are forever grateful to her and her lovely husband Fred, who not only nurtured him, but also us as we evolved as parents. It was the first special bond our son made with another person outside of our immediate family, and we are eternally grateful to her for giving us faith in childcare.

With the need for childcare a couple of days a week now pressing, having heard of friends' positive experiences with nurseries, we decided to have a look at a few of the recommended ones locally. Again, before I'd had my son, I was adamant that I would never put my son into day care – and yet again, I was surprised by my ever-changing perspective on things.

We settled on a lovely traditional nursery literally five minutes away from our home. Our positive experience with Pauline still did little to curb my nerves and anxiety at leaving him on his first day, though, aged nine months exactly. His settling-in sessions had gone well, but seeing his little face crumple with bewilderment when I left him that first day was like a dagger to my heart. Children's carers are so well versed in knowing how to cope with emotional parents – I think I got as many cuddles as my boy!

It didn't help either that some opinionated old trout in the bank queue afterwards commented on my tear-stained face, and when I explained that I was a bit emotional having just dropped my son off at nursery, she TUTTED and told me he 'should be at home with me anyway'. It took a great deal of self-control not to flick her on the forehead and stab her cold unfeeling heart with the freebie miniature biro I was holding. Never let anyone make you feel crap about your choices. They really have no idea!

Without exception, ALL of my mum friends have spoken (and cried) about the gut-wrenching feelings of leaving their kids at nursery those first few times. As time has gone on I have learned to cope with drop-off much better, and this is definitely due to the fact that not only do we have no tears any more (from either of us), but the minute we arrive, Enzo can't wait to get down from me and get stuck in to all the fun activities and endless snacks – I barely get a backwards glance, and if I do, it's one that consists of a big gummy smile, and his newly learned 'baby wave' goodbye. We have asked a lot of him, but he is a happy and settled little boy, and we couldn't be more pleased with the choices we've made for him so far – so trout-face-bank-woman can bugger off!

'We've just made the decision that I'm not going to go back to work. It is quite a tough one but I don't want to go to work just to be able to cover the costs of childcare – I feel I'd rather be with my baby and see her grow up than go back to only coming home with a few hundred pounds after the costs of childcare and travel have been taken care of.'

Bryony – mum to Giada, aged 10 months

Some people enlist the help of grandparents (it can often be the cheapest and preferred option), or childminders, nannies, au pairs, or as we have, private nurseries. Most options are expensive and can be a source of financial anxiety in themselves, so it's always a good idea to talk through all the options available to you to work out what might be the best idea overall for you and your family.

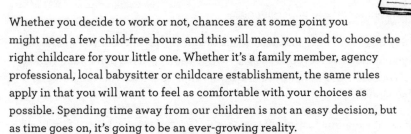

Be a detective

Whether you decide to work or not, chances are at some point you might need a few child-free hours and this will mean you need to choose the right childcare for your little one. Whether it's a family member, agency professional, local babysitter or childcare establishment, the same rules apply in that you will want to feel as comfortable with your choices as possible. Spending time away from our children is not an easy decision, but as time goes on, it's going to be an ever-growing reality.

Do your detective work early, ask questions and research all options to ensure you're as clued up as possible about who you choose to care for your precious little person. You also may well need to get your name on a waiting list as early as possible, so it pays to do the research early on.

Get recommendations and ask friends and family if they have tried-and-tested childcare options – word of mouth is always a good starting point.

Explore childcare that matches your ideals and values, such as that it is homely, cosy, quiet, promotes healthy eating, uses routines, follows an educational or development plan etc.

Interview! Whoever you might choose to join your family in looking after your child, make sure you get to know them as best you can first. Have a coffee meeting, go to a meet-and-greet session, visit the nursery and speak to the manager and other parents. Find out everything you want to know and ask any important questions – if they're any good, they won't mind – rather they'll welcome it!

Do your research – the internet can be a help in finding out any further information you might like to know. Ofsted is the national governing body for standards in education, children's services and skills. They will disclose information about any nursery you're looking into. Your local council can advise you of registered childminders in your area. Ask any childcarer you're thinking of using if they have first-aid skills and are DBS (Disclosure and Barring Service) registered – this all helps to ensure someone's suitability, skillset, safety and professionalism.

Say what you want – and don't want. You are the parent so if you would like your child to be rocked to sleep, a routine kept to, or you don't want them to have sugar, for example, you have every right to ask for your wishes to be adhered to.

Go with your gut instinct. If someone isn't right for you and your family, then it's perfectly OK to choose someone else. Your child's well-being comes first. Always.

Coping with separation anxiety

Separation anxiety occurs when a person experiences excessive anxiety regarding separation from home or from people they have a strong emotional attachment to, for example, a parent, caregiver or siblings. Although separation anxiety is a perfectly normal part of childhood, it can be very unsettling and upsetting for both the child and the parent.

Understanding what your child is going through and having a few coping strategies can really help both of you get through it.

Babies up to the age of six months tend to settle more easily than a child approaching a year old. This is simply due to developmental milestones – a slightly older baby has become more aware of mummy or daddy leaving, even if only into the other room. They may cry, become agitated and clingy when you start to leave, but in the main these symptoms don't last for too long, and as awful as it can feel when you say goodbye, the chances are that your baby has calmed down and been helpfully distracted by the time you've reached the front door.

Try to view the positives in that any sign of separation anxiety from either you or your child means that a healthy bond has developed, and any feelings of guilt just show you care.

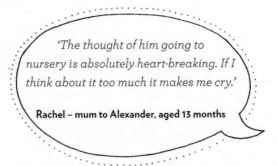

'The thought of him going to nursery is absolutely heart-breaking. If I think about it too much it makes me cry.'

Rachel – mum to Alexander, aged 13 months

Help make leaving your child a little easier for you both by being consistent with your actions. Your little one needs to build up trust and confidence in you, so when you leave, be firm, loving and actively communicate with a kiss and cuddle, and follow through with leaving (coming straight back or delaying will only cause more confusion and distress), and then make sure you return when you say you will. Children take time to adjust to new surroundings and routines, but by being calm and consistent, listening to your child and going with your instinct, there's every chance you'll nip any separation anxiety in the bud in no time at all. And remember, you are not alone – you can go and weep with the other mums once you are out of sight of the front door!

How to handle goodbyes

TRY TO arrive on time – not too early and not too late – so that you have time to take off their coat, hang up their bag and hand them to their key carer (almost all nurseries have these) without any sense of stress that you are running late, or hanging about to wait for the key carer to be ready to receive them.

MAKE SURE they have their favourite comfort toy with them and sleeping bag (or whatever bedding you have at home) if they still take day naps. This will make them feel much more secure in the new environment, and is invaluable if they get upset later in the day even if they seem fine at drop-off.

GIVE THEM one kiss and cuddle, smile and say 'have a great day, I'll see you at x o'clock', and then walk out of the door without looking back. It feels hideous at first but it's important not to 'sneak' out as this can leave your child feeling anxious and confused about where you've gone. They might cry initially (and it's completely ok if you do in the car afterwards too), but it's better for them to recover quickly from knowing you've gone and are coming back, than to spend the day wondering and potentially worrying.

WHEN THEY are with you, make sure you speak only in positive terms about the childcare setting, and be really enthusiastic about all the fun things they get to do there and the friendships they have made.

AT PICK UP time make sure you give your little one a cuddle, be enthusiastic, vocally proud and interested in what they've accomplished during the day – your child will be excited to share the day to day activities with you.

Dr Reetta says...

The thorny question of work

Whatever you decide about going back to work, or not, there is no simple set of instructions or definite answers about what will be best for you and your baby. It is about working it out to the best of your ability as you go through it, trying to balance all of your needs as a family. Real 'choices' may be limited due to the complexity of individual family needs, workplace needs and finances. Parenting guides that push a prescribed way forwards have no chance of capturing the richness and complexity of an individual family's experience. Something that often comes up in research and in my own clinical work, and as Anna and her husband are experiencing, is that many of today's parents would like to combine parenthood and work but many are faced with the dilemma of devoting themselves to *either* work *or* their children, not both.

Everybody's needs are different – and it also depends how flexible your work is. On top of that you have a baby with a unique temperament. You may have a high-needs baby, who reacts intensely to changes and separation, and only seems happy in your arms. It can feel overwhelming having to even think about work and childcare. As with other areas of parenting, there aren't any guarantees nor is there a magic formula to make this transition easy, but there are some things you can do (see tips 2 and 3) to make it smoother.

Separation anxiety is a phase in your child's development. Often the worst of it occurs between nine and twelve months, which is coincidentally right when many mothers are returning to work, but it can continue until the age of three, or later. It may return when your child is sick or under stress, or at later stages of childhood, such as when they are starting school or going back after the holidays.

Dealing with decisions about work and separation from your baby

1. Dana Breen, a renowned psychoanalyst and author, talks about 'the hurdle model' in her book *Talking with Mothers*. This is when a person prepares to and then does overcome a difficulty and how life afterwards goes back to normal – think about when you have overcome hurdles with education and work, preparing for exams, job interviews, presentations – and then have relaxed afterwards. As Breen points out, becoming a mother is not like that (and I would add, the same goes for many fathers.) Women and men may have done a lot of preparation for the birth and got through it, but what they are faced with afterwards doesn't follow the same model – there won't be any period of relaxation after the big event! Instead, there will be hurdle after hurdle, whatever you do in regards to work and childcare. Anna says 'trust in change and allow it to settle down'. I would add: try to embrace chaos and difference, or however life looks like now, compared to how it looked before parenthood. This will soon become your 'new normal'.

2. Whether you are going back to work or not, there will be times when you are going to be separated from your child. If you are reluctant to separate it reinforces the fear of separation in your child. It is common for parents to try to avoid 'causing' their child any worry or upset. At the same time, feeling slightly upset when leaving your child is normal. However, with separation anxiety some things that parents do can cause the child's anxiety to get bigger. Have a think: is there anything about how you approach separation (your body language, tone of voice, what you say) that you would like to try to change?

3. Although it's hard to leave your child with a caregiver while they're distressed, as Anna says, there is a positive aspect to separation anxiety: it can indicate a healthy attachment between you and your child! Teach your child that people do return: playing Peek a Boo, Hide and Seek and reading books in which people come back can be helpful with this. Some of my favourite children's books on this topic are: *The Kissing Hand* by Audrey Penn, *Mama Always Comes Home* by Karma Wilson, *Llama Llama Misses Mama* by Anna Dewdney, and *The Invisible String* by Patrice Karst.

'Prior to having my baby I had a set plan that nine months' maternity leave would be sufficient, that I would feel comfortable returning to work full time (across four days) and happy leaving her in the care of someone else. Since spending that time together and bonding this is by far my biggest anxiety.'

Marta – mum to Olivia, aged 12 months

8
IT'S NOT JUST MUM
The 'don't forget dad' feeling

 It's much easier to become a father than to be one.

Kent Nerburn, *Letters to My Son,* **1999**

Baby steps...

YOU MATTER TOO. You may not have physically given birth to your new baby but you are equally as important, and that goes for your feelings, too.

IT TAKES TIME to adjust to your new dad role. Like mum, there is a period of change and settling in... Don't rush and just take each day as it comes.

LET IT OUT! Men in particular can keep their thoughts and feelings to themselves, but this won't help anyone, least of all you. Confide in your partner, friend or someone you trust and let any negativity or worry out.

One for the dads

Hands up if you're a mum, and as you read the title of this particular chapter you did a little snort of contempt at the mere *suggestion* that guys might have it hard when it comes to parenting. I've lost count of the amount of times people have ribbed my husband when he's complained about how hard raising a child can be, and I must admit, I do often sneer whenever a dose of man-flu threatens an appearance – which *obviously* renders him incapable of daddy duties while he snivels as though he's at death's door for days on end.

But eye rolling aside, dads obviously matter too. Gone are the days when an expectant father nervously propped up the local boozer smoking cigars, while his wife did all the hard work in the nearest maternity ward. We have come a long way from those clichéd, segregated roles, and more than ever parenting is as wonderfully diverse as I believe it should be.

Dads are just as important, and vulnerable, in their new parenting role as anyone. So dads, this is a chapter all about you. Your thoughts, feelings and behaviours as you embark on the crazy journey of being a parent, and for us mums, a chance to explore and listen to what might be going on for the baby-daddies in our lives – *without* us pulling rank for once.

> *'It was on one random Thursday night after work in the pub with my pregnant fiancée at home, and it all started sinking in – the guilt, the worry, the regret and my first proper moment of anxiety: sh*t I'm going to be a dad!'*
>
> **Daniel – dad to Willow, aged 12 months**

Becoming dad

For obvious reasons this chapter has proved to be one of the most challenging to write, so as well as conducting my own research, tapping up my husband and giving him carte blanche to offload, I've also put my little black book to work and enlisted the help of some of my wonderful dad pals to assist me in ensuring I get down to the nitty gritty, and represent men properly.

The overwhelming feedback I get from dads is that the shift from happy-go-lucky guy to responsible parent is huge. There is so much focus on the mums, and understandably so, but often new fathers feel sidelined, disregarded and yet just as equally terrified about the monumental life change that becoming a parent brings. Post-natal depression and anxiety in dads is rarely talked about, but I can assure you, it's a thing, and something that should be treated with as much respect and concern as it is for anyone else. Witnessing your child coming into the world from a dad's perspective is one of the most emotionally charged, tense and surreal moments a man can ever experience, and OK, they might not have done the physical birthing bit, but it can be equally traumatic and have lasting emotional and mental effects that may need addressing. We'll be exploring post-natal depression and anxiety in dads a little later in this chapter.

> *'I think the realisation that you're responsible for a life suddenly dawns on you – it's a very lonely period.'*
>
> **Ben – dad to Darcy, aged three months**

Nowadays, I'd say the majority of fathers are present at the birth of their babies – expectant mums want them there for the practical and emotional support. From attending antenatal classes and panic buying unnecessary baby paraphernalia to cheering their partner on at the bedside, guys on the whole are very much involved in assisting in their offspring's arrival – in fact the NCT reports that a whopping 97 per cent of dads are present at the birth of their child these days. Of course, however, some mothers do prefer their baby's father not to be present, choosing instead a birth partner such as a family member, friend or professional doula. What's more, interestingly, a survey carried out by the Royal College of Midwives showed that a significant number of mothers (over one-third) wished their partner hadn't been present, with many saying they 'got in the way'.

Compared to the varying degrees of pain, compromised dignity and exhaustion often experienced by the mother, the birth-partner dad role does seem like the far easier and preferred choice. Hell, I'd have preferred to be the flannel-toting bystander at my son's birth! However, the lack of control that some guys report can feel just as intense emotionally and mentally.

If my husband could have switched places with me throughout my pregnancy and labour I'm certain he would have. Easy to say, but I know that the lack of control he felt while watching me in distress, and knowing that our baby was in a tricky position, was the most stressful and anxious time of his life. At one point he had a genuine fear of losing both of us (he was wrong, by the way – the docs had it all under control, I can assure you), but he still speaks emotionally of feeling redundant in the operating theatre as several medics took over, wiring me up to machines, asking for my consent to carry out emergency 'procedures', while he sat hopelessly in a chair 'all gowned up with nowhere to go'. It was his wife. His baby. And although he appreciated that I was in good hands, he was also well aware that he didn't have a CLUE about what was happening, or if everything was going to be OK. I can only imagine the fear he must have felt in those tense few minutes, having no choice but to simply go along with how his son was about to be born, and praying no one would cock it up.

Prior to the birth, we'd had a 'deal' about how I was to find out the sex of our baby… I had envisaged this romantic scene where my husband would assist in the final 'bit' and present our new son or daughter to me. We'd cry tears of joy, pose for pics and snuggle together as a new little family of three, like they sometimes do on *One Born Every Minute*. The reality was that he had to witness his baby being yanked out of me rather forcefully by forceps, (which, let's just say, was messy), he saw a little bundle of baby boy 'bits' dangling as the obstetrician held him aloft, and tearfully whispered to me 'Anna, we've got a boy'. I was so shocked and out of it by this point that my poor other half had to savour this life-affirming moment solo, and as I lay there in recovery, my husband suddenly had the terrifying responsibility of needing to tend to our new baby, while also not wanting to leave my side. He admits now that the whole experience knocked him for six, and for several weeks afterwards he felt in a state of shock and very emotional.

'Most people would say that the birth of their child is the happiest moment of their life. I love my new baby dearly and I was on cloud nine when he was born and for the first few months of his life, but now I'm ashamed to find myself overcome with anxiety and depression during what should be such a fun time.'

Phil – dad to Zachary, aged six months

Daddy doubts

Much like new mums, dads report major insecurities about being 'good enough'. Why do we all heap so much pressure and expectation on ourselves? Well, it's because we care. Most of us strive to be the best parent possible from the moment the test shows positive, but it's safe to say that many fathers completely crap themselves the moment they become one.

One of the initial anxieties seems to relate to the practicalities of parenting. How do I know what to do? Will I be able to do everything? Will the baby like me? Will I like the baby back? All of these are real concerns from real dads. By far the most talked-about cause of sheer panic experienced in those fledgling days, though, is the dreaded 'nappy anxiety'.

Let's be honest chaps, other than ensuring one's own pants are changed on a (vaguely) regular basis, handling bodily fluids and excrement is pretty much a solo activity. Women have their monthly joy to deal with, but guys, other than the morning 'sh*t, shower, shave', sequence, that really is about as down and dirty as it gets – that is, until a little poo monster moves in.

The moment you become a dad, it is pretty much expected in this day and age that you'll roll your sleeves up and get well and truly stuck in to the nappy-changing shit storm. Gone are the days when chaps can duck out of the rota. In fact, during those early few weeks in particular while mum is recovering and needing a break in between feeds, it's often over to daddy to do the honours.

My husband was actually the first to change our son's nappy in the hospital. I was gratefully slurping away at my tea and munching my toast post birth when the 'don't mess with me' midwife bowled over to our cubicle and instructed us that we needed to change the baby's nappy. Happy to be useful and carry out his first daddy job, my other half enthusiastically followed instructions as he cautiously opened up the pooey Pandora's Box... Yet little did he know quite how stubborn the first meconium poo can be. You know the one I'm talking about yeah? Like a bit of chewing gum stuck on your shoe, it just won't come off unless some serious effort is put in.

Minute after minute went by as attempts to remove the sticky tar-like substance were unsuccessful. The more he wiped, the more the wretched stuff spread like Marmite. Watched over by me, the midwife and goodness knows who else's prying eyes, I'm surprised the poor bloke didn't just throw in the towel, declare 'sod this', and just bail for the door sharpish! In his words, the moment he'd completed this gruelling task he felt 'bloody relieved' – until the next time a poonami struck that is.

Nappy 'anxiety' (I use the term loosely here as it's more a knackered, can't-be-arsed stress than actual anxiety) inflicts itself on us all... nobody enjoys the sweat-inducing gamble of nappy-changing time, and parents all over the world are in a constant battle of 'no, it's YOUR turn!' I know my husband and I aren't the only ones who make impassioned pleas to each other of 'why can't *you* do it?', and pull rock, paper, scissors to get out of the unpleasant job – the winner literally jumping for joy at dodging a grouchy, kicking, squirming, screaming banshee. I can only imagine the JOY that successful potty training brings, signalling the end of nappy anxiety forever.

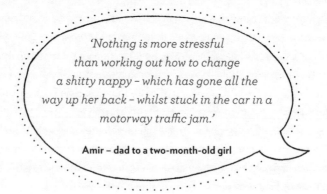

'Nothing is more stressful than working out how to change a shitty nappy – which has gone all the way up her back – whilst stuck in the car in a motorway traffic jam.'

Amir – dad to a two-month-old girl

A lot of fathers take paternity leave, some don't, occasionally some go it alone as single dads, and others decide to take on, or share, the parenting with their partner. This latter is what my husband and I decided to do. The nature of our work is such that no two weeks are the same, and that's also true when it comes to our income. As I've explained in earlier chapters, the need for me to resume some sort of normality with work became fairly immediately apparent, so we made an agreement to share the childcare duties between us as best we could.

Stay-at-home dads are on the rise: the Office of National Statistics reports that the amount of fathers who are the main childcare provider has doubled in the last 20 years. There are around a quarter of a million chaps in the UK who are now raising their kids while their partner goes out to work. A recent survey carried out by insurer Aviva shows that one in seven dads are the main childcare providers in UK households, and nearly a quarter of dads either give up work or reduce their hours after the birth of their children. What seems to be pretty certain is that stay-at-home dads, although not the majority, are definitely growing in numbers.

Many factors dictate whether or not a father takes on the Daddy Day Care role – most commonly it's for financial reasons, and if a partner is earning more it can often seem like the sensible option for one parent to work and the other to take on the day-to-day task of raising the kids.

Being a part-time, or full-time dad, can carry its own stresses, anxieties and stigma. Some guys report feeling emasculated, judged and lonely, and it's an unfair and upsetting burden to carry. But in the age of equality, it is definitely, and thankfully, lifting, with a load of guys taking the (baby) reins and proudly becoming the primary carer.

It can of course be a nerve-wracking role at first, but my husband now has no problem taking our son to rhyme time, baby signing, or Enzo's weekly SwimKidz class – he's not ashamed or embarrassed to grovel around on the floor pretending to be a 'horsey', and he can belt out *Old Macdonald* better than anyone (in fact he can sing it in both English AND Italian). The really fab thing is he's not the only man at these gatherings. OK, it's mostly mums, but there are always one or two other dads giving it some welly too – and I can guarantee you they are made to feel welcome. In fact the dads at my son's groups are often the leaders in the 'shall we all go for a coffee and play date after class?' idea. We're all one and the same – parents in need of coffee and chat.

So, if you're a dad who's getting stuck into childcare, first, good for you, and second, you're not alone in the slightest. There are dad groups popping up all over the shop, on social media, locally to you, via ante/post-natal groups etc, so why not have a look around at who you might be able to buddy up with, hone your best soft-play game, and embrace an extremely worthwhile job. These websites are especially great for dads: www.dad.info and www.fatherhoodinstitute.org, containing a wealth of tips, information and advice on how to be an involved father, whether you are the primary carer or not.

In contrast to the above scenario, there are many dads who aren't able to spend as much time with their child/ren as they'd like. Perhaps you and the mum aren't together, or your working hours/location mean your time is limited with your baby, or maybe you feel unsure how to fit in in understanding your new role. Whatever your situation, it's important that you don't bottle it up and plod along in silence. Make the most of the time you do have with your little one and ensure you factor in opportunities to be 'daddy'. If you travel a lot, Facetime and Skype can be really helpful for keeping in touch with your family if you're unable to be there in person, and can be very effective when it comes to keeping the contact and familiarity with your baby as close as possible.

'My job as a flight attendant takes me away from home for several nights a month and I'm often exhausted and jet-lagged when I return. I find it difficult to fit back into the family dynamic, and know what to do with my daughter as all the routines and phases seem to evolve weekly! I've started making sure I have a whole day of just daddy-daughter time to make sure we keep bonding.'

James – dad to Molly, aged six months

How to... be the best you can be

PERHAPS you're not able to be around as much as you'd like, or you're feeling a bit left out in your new dad role. It's important to speak up and tell your partner/the baby's mum how you feel – they aren't a mind reader so share your feelings with them.

ASK FOR help and to be included as much as possible. If you're unsure of how to do some things, such as feeding or nappy changing, ask for some extra support and guidance. It will help in building up your confidence and self-esteem as a new dad.

SUGGEST TIMES when you're around and free to spend quality time with your baby, and as a family. If it helps, or works for you, treat it like a work or doctor's appointment and block it out of your diary as 'highly important'.

CHOOSE something special to do regularly with your child, a daddy-baby activity such as a walk, reading a story or bath time. The routine will do wonders for you both and be something to look forward to.

MAKE THE time you DO spend with your little one count. Put your phone and laptop away, turn off the TV and just enjoy spending uninterrupted time together, playing, talking and having cuddles.

DO WHAT you can to keep in touch and present in your child/ren's life. If you're away from the house use Facetime, Skype or the phone to keep in contact so you can see and hear each other regularly. Read stories, ask questions, make silly noises, and sing songs... whatever you feel like to keep that connection and bond strong. That way, out of sight is NOT out of mind.

IF YOU HAVE more than one child, one of the most useful things you can do is make a bit of a fuss of the other children, who may well be feeling a bit miffed, and try to make things as normal for them as possible by doing stuff you enjoyed before the new baby came along.

When paternity leave... leaves

It seems like only moments ago you were vegging out on the sofa cradling your newborn among the congratulatory chaos of cards, flowers and presents, and in the blink of a sleep-deprived eye, the couple of weeks' paternity leave is over and most chaps find themselves back at work. However, 'work' is no longer just where you go to earn a crust, and gone are the days when you can hotfoot it straight to the pub for a pint, the gym for a session, or even straight home for a chill on the couch.

For dads who return to work after the birth of their baby, it can suddenly feel like the work/home-life balance is more than a little compromised, and all seems to roll into one. Loads of new fathers describe it as feeling as though the workload has doubled overnight.

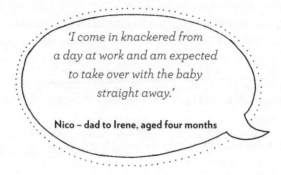

'I come in knackered from a day at work and am expected to take over with the baby straight away.'

Nico – dad to Irene, aged four months

Competitive tiredness is a new parent's trump card. Those first few weeks and months in particular are a constant tug of war of who deserves to be the most knackered. Sure, mum may have been at home all day caring for a temperamental energy thief, but for a working dad, the financial responsibility suddenly felt at needing to provide for his new family, dealing with the same old work demands but on broken sleep, feelings of guilt at not being at home to help with the baby, coping with a frazzled partner, and then busting a gut to get back for bath time, can make even the strongest of chaps falter. Despite what the mum mags and forums might say – in jest, or not – both new and old-hand dads, on the whole, do not have it easy, and the anxiety, pressure and fear of f**king up is all too real.

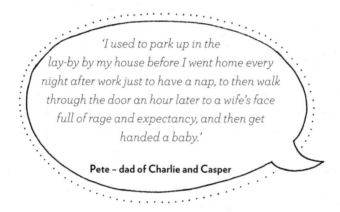

'I used to park up in the lay-by by my house before I went home every night after work just to have a nap, to then walk through the door an hour later to a wife's face full of rage and expectancy, and then get handed a baby.'

Pete – dad of Charlie and Casper

Add to this pressure cooker of stress an exhausted hormonal partner, perhaps a chaotic house, perhaps other tired children, and more often than not an empty fridge – right at the time you all need it magically stocked full of your favourite comfort food – it's a breeding ground for grouchy bad-temperedness. When I asked my hubby for his comments for this chapter, he reminisced with an almost painful look in his eye at 'the hunger' and need of a 'decent meal' – he wasn't expecting me to knock one up for him, he is actually the cook in our house, but he was too knackered to even bother. For the first few months we lived on microwave meals, crisps and toast.

They say that in the lead-up to having a baby you should stock up your freezer with meals so that you're all set once you've battened down the hatches in those early weeks – I really wished we'd listened to that stellar advice. Well, we sort of did, but given I was two weeks overdue, we'd already eaten most of our over-eager trolley-dash supplies by the time our boy arrived, so we ended up going home from the hospital to an off pint of milk and half a packet of pasta shells.

Fill The Freezer !!!

An army marches on its stomach, and never has that saying been truer for parents of newborns. Never underestimate how much good a decent meal can do – being 'hangry' is not fun for anyone. While mums and dads understandably prioritise the baby, we have to be careful not to let our own health go down the drain, and if we have other children then they still need to eat nutritious meals, at normal times. Grabbing a slice of toast in between feeds, or gorging on Jaffa Cakes, after a while only adds to the general feeling of crapness, and you just end up feeling so tired and hungry that it only serves to fuel arguments. The other half and I had some absolute whoppers in the first few weeks, and he admits that forgetting to eat properly, and therefore having sod all patience, motivation or energy to do anything properly, was largely to blame.

We eventually asked my parents to watch the baby at mealtimes sometimes, just so we could ensure we ate proper food every few days – I cannot tell you how much good that seemingly small act did for our sanity and marriage! Of course for the vast majority of people this simply isn't an option, however, do read up on (there are a gazillion web pages devoted to the topic) cunning ways to very quickly and easily rustle up decent grub while dangling a howling newborn, listening to your three-year-old's account of their day painting sticks and gluing recycling together to make a 'train', and hanging out the washing. Doing an online supermarket shop at 2am is also a great use of your time – just avoid the chocolate biscuit section and try not to accidentally order 20 packets of bacon rather than two.

Breaking Point

S.O.S

TALK TO your boss and colleagues if you're feeling the heat from being back at work and struggling on no sleep. You might be able to have a power nap in your lunch break or have responsibility eased off you for a bit. They most likely have been there – or will be some day too!

MAKE SURE you eat! It can be the most obvious of things we forget to do, but eating and drinking good nutritious food and beverages is important to help support your physical, emotional and mental well-being – and not just breastfeeding mums. Lay off too much anxiety-inducing coffee and sugar-laden treats, and instead stock up on hearty soups, salads and wholegrain low-GI carbs that slowly release their energy and help you avoid blood-sugar level spikes.

IF THE BABY'S crying, your other half is moaning and it's all getting too much... instead of blowing your top, walk calmly away/outside/to the bottom of the garden/another room, count to ten slowly and rejoin when the anger and frustration has reduced.

Running the mummy gauntlet

One of the best quotes I was given, by a dad of three about him and his wife was: 'we wistfully dreamed of family outings, enjoying quality time and making memories together.' This was said while on their summer holiday, with dripping sarcasm and an almost vacant look in the eye as he grappled with two of his three children having a scrap over his smartphone. The other one sat sulkily in the corner shouting repeatedly 'I want to go home', while the wife gratefully guzzled wine at the opposite end of the restaurant, leaving him to it. Interestingly, this exasperation was echoed by quite a few chaps who couldn't wait to offload their gripes and groans for this book.

It's a rare dad who is spared the wrath of their new-baby mother, and in the words of many, 'what the hell has she turned into?!' I know for sure that my husband thought his normally happy-go-lucky (if a little hyper) wife had turned into a mercurial nightmare... angry one minute, terrifying the next... with a few emotional outbursts thrown in. It was tough for him, but selfishly at the time, I just couldn't fathom any hardship he might have been feeling, I was too consumed in my own emotional rollercoaster – and this is a dangerous path to take. A couple needs to work as a team, particularly when there's a baby in the mix. No one 'gets off lightly'.

> *'The fun moments definitely outweigh the dark moments, I think it's nature's clever way of making you forget the crap bits.'*
>
> **Sam – dad to Joseph, aged two years**

New dads are expected to be mind readers... What would she like/need/want? The answer is always sleep. Lots of uninterrupted sleep. But let's be fair, that's all dads want and need too. But other than this fabled promised land of peace and tranquility where no one is nagging at you, there are also worries of how to soothe the baby, how to deal with the dreaded colic, what to do if little one has a temperature, how the hell does one of those ruddy baby thermometers even work (!), can we use Calpol yet, does my wife need a cuddle, will she yell at me if I go near her...? The questions and concerns are endless, and the overall pressure of just keeping your new baby alive, and your relationship out of a divorce court, is one hell of a task – and pressure.

It's tricky to get definitive statistics on break-ups and divorce following the birth of a baby, but parenting go-to-resource, *Babble*, suggests that one in six couples divorce within five years of the birth of a first child. Two-thirds of couples say the quality of their relationship declined in the first three years of having children. The Marriage Foundation, which analysed figures from the National Office of Statistics, says that almost half of all 16-year-olds will have experienced a family split at some time from birth onwards. Whatever the facts and figures, these stats aren't meant to depress. Use them as a positive heads-up to guard against any parenting angst and agro, and instead develop ways to keep your relationship healthy and intact. It can feel a bit cheesy to have date nights and talk about your feelings, but trust me, the benefits are invaluable. Get these practices nailed now, and you'll be more likely to be sorted.

> *'I find I have longer showers as it's the only time I get for some peace and quiet – or when I'm on the toilet having a poo.'*
>
> **Steve – dad to Stanley, aged six months**

Getting to know you

Even the healthiest of relationships can be strained by the addition of a new baby. Couples can be tested, new or extra responsibilities and demands can cause even the most solid of parents to buckle under the pressure and result in some of the most almighty arguments.

In general, when it is 'just' new baby stress, the situation tends to improve dramatically when the couple is able to get more sleep and spend time together without biting each other's head off.

Signs to be aware of that might flag something more troubling in your relationship can include a dramatic and lasting shift in behaviour, such as constant arguing, and avoiding spending time together, perhaps preferring to stay late at work, or in the pub.

Try this simple activity to reconnect with your partner and remember what you like and love about each other.

- Find a moment when it's calm and quiet when you can give each other undivided attention for a few minutes.

Write down five things you like about your partner, and have them do the same.

- Taking it in turns, read out your 'like lists' to each other, appreciating what each other has said.

If there is any conflict or niggles, add to the list 'one thing I would like you to change' and in turn reflect and discuss in a positive and unchallenging way how this might be actioned. If there is a worry this might get in any way heated or turn into a row, then it's a good idea to ask someone (friend, family member, or even a counsellor) to sit in the room with you to act as a non-judgemental mediator. Compromising and allowing the other to talk is key here. If it gets narky in any way, agree to walk away for a few moments to gather yourselves and breathe, before returning and resuming the chat in a calm fashion.

Keep checking in each week to see how the list/s might change and evolve, adding or taking away anything that would benefit your relationship and 'same page' thinking.

If you find this tricky in any way, consider writing each other a letter in which you can offload your feelings and wishes in an unchallenged and uninterrupted way. Writing things down can be hugely cathartic, and is a helpful way to communicate without arguing.

Piggy in the middle

There's arguably more and more support out there nowadays for new mums – drop-in centres, coffee mornings, support groups and, in my case, my trusted WhatsApp group of fellow new mums, always on call to soothe any moment of panic I might be experiencing. Dads, on the whole, feel that there is much less available to them and that they are just expected to suck it up.

Many also report the classic feeling of being redundant or a spare part during the first few weeks and months following their baby's birth. The new mum's mother (ie granny – the mother-in-law – duh duh duh!!) seems to be a big talking point and a bone of contention among new-parent couples, with over-enthusiastic grandmas – or indeed those who are not being helpful enough – a bit of a battle ground as support roles are defined.

My husband felt some level of being pushed out from the labour into the first few weeks as I needed my mum around me so much. He felt I preferred her to him, and to be honest, he was probably right. It was almost as if I'd regressed back to being a child myself as I just wanted my own mum to help soothe me and tell me it was all going to be alright.

It wasn't that my husband was crap or uncaring, he was great, but I guess that primal instinct just took over for both her and me, as she helped me through the biggest life change I'd ever had to experience. And as a mother of three kids herself, she was far better placed to help me adjust than anyone else. My mother-in-law was also extremely helpful (a mother of three, too), and in those early, anxiety-wracked weeks, she would also offer me invaluable and non-judgemental advice and support to help me get the hang of how the hell to be a mum.

Talking and communicating about how you feel is key. If you're feeling in any way left out or sidelined, do confide in those who matter – it can really help to redress the balance of where you fit in.

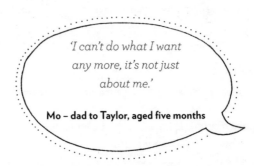

'I can't do what I want any more, it's not just about me.'

Mo – dad to Taylor, aged five months

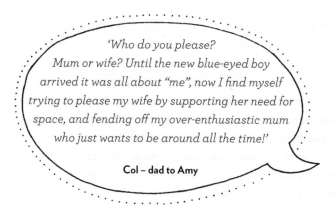

'Who do you please?
Mum or wife? Until the new blue-eyed boy
arrived it was all about "me", now I find myself
trying to please my wife by supporting her need for
space, and fending off my over-enthusiastic mum
who just wants to be around all the time!'

Col – dad to Amy

Some men shared their experiences of how it feels being the only dad in their group of friends, or perhaps the first one at work to become a parent. So many of them told me that 'non-baby friends just don't get it', and speak of feeling lonely when mates are cracking on with their happy-go-lucky lives. As one dad reported: 'people just don't get that you can't just drop everything and come to the pub as you're at home with the baby and in an unbreakable routine'. Others talk of feelings of FOMO (fear of missing out) if you're the first among peers to have kids.

Remember chaps, everyone experiences similar feelings, mums too – you are totally not alone and it's super important to keep up with your mates as best you're able, even via text or the odd social media banter, just to give yourself some much-needed bloke company away from nappies and hormones.

For every mum of a newborn, there is also a dad, so take comfort in the fact that most guys are going through the motions too, enduring the sleep challenges and life change, so next time you see a fellow dad in the supermarket check-out queue, or wrestling a tantruming toddler into a buggy, give him a knowing smile safe in the knowledge that he and you are not alone in the slightest. Also take a moment to remind yourself what an incredible thing you have entered into – you have created a human being, and chances are, if they haven't already, most of your mates will follow suit eventually, and then you can be the smug Know It All, ha ha. Be proud of your dad role, you're smashing it.

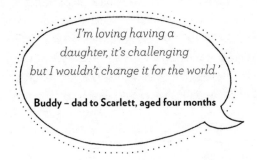

'I'm loving having a daughter, it's challenging but I wouldn't change it for the world.'

Buddy – dad to Scarlett, aged four months

I'm a New Dad Get Me Outta Here! – PND in dads

OK, so I've talked about post-natal depression, anxiety and birth trauma for new mums in previous chapters, so here we'll shed a little bit of light on how these same conditions can also be experienced by dads. Post-natal mental health issues in fathers is a big deal. Time to put stigma and embarrassment in a box, lock it and throw away the key.

'My wife successfully delivered our little girl a few weeks ago. She is happy, healthy and I absolutely love her, but I can't seem to shake my anxiety over being a new father. I feel guilty about feeling so anxious because I love my little girl, my wife, and the fact that we are raising a child together.'

Chris – dad to Emily, aged three weeks

Just as with new mums, according to the NCT, up to 1 in 10 new dads experience post-natal depression and anxiety and that figure is higher for parents of multiples or children with a disability. If it's going to happen, it's likely to creep up during the first year after having a baby (but it can sometimes hit later too, and is not by any means restricted to first-time parents), and it can happen gradually or all of a sudden, and can range from relatively mild to serious.

Research from the NCT found that more than one in three new fathers (38 per cent) are concerned about their mental health, and in general, fathers appear to be more likely to suffer from depression three to six months after their baby is born.

There are lots of things you can do to recognise the symptoms and indeed help ease them.

Causes of post-natal depression and anxiety (sometimes called paternal depression and anxiety) in fathers include:

- A stressful, unsettling or emotionally traumatic life event (so having a baby can be all of these!);
- Financial responsibility;
- Changes in relationship and lifestyle;
- Lack of sleep;
- Increased workload – both at home and work;
- Concerns about partner and/or baby.

A strained relationship with your partner during the pregnancy can also have an effect after the baby is born, and a partner who has had, or is experiencing, depression and anxiety, can also have an impact.

Younger dads are particularly susceptible to low mood and higher rates of anxiety and depression, as well as fathers on a low income. Other things to consider are past mental health issues, social factors such as culture and religion, and family history.

Symptoms of post-natal depression and anxiety to be aware of include:

- Feeling very low, or despondent, that life is a long, grey tunnel, and that there is no hope.
- Feeling tired and very lethargic, or even quite numb.
- Not wanting to do anything or take an interest in the outside world.
- Feeling a sense of inadequacy or unable to cope.
- Feeling guilty about not coping, or about not loving the baby enough.
- Being unusually irritable, which makes the guilt worse.
- Wanting to cry/crying a lot or even constantly.
- Having obsessive and irrational thoughts that can be very scary.
- Loss of appetite, which may go with feeling hungry all the time, but being unable to eat.
- Comfort eating.
- Having difficulty sleeping: either not getting to sleep, waking early, or having vivid nightmares.
- Being hostile or indifferent to your partner and/or baby.
- Having panic attacks, which strike at any time, causing a rapid heartbeat, sweaty palms and feelings of sickness or faintness.
- Having an overpowering anxiety, often about things that wouldn't normally bother you, such as being alone in the house.
- Having difficulty in concentrating or making decisions.
- Experiencing physical symptoms, such as headaches.
- Having obsessive fears about your baby's health or well-being, or about yourself and other members of the family.
- Having disturbing thoughts about harming yourself or your baby.
- Having thoughts about death.

If you're experiencing any of these feelings, please do not panic, the main thing is that you talk about it. Keeping it all inside won't help, whereas talking to your partner, GP, or looking into a support group via Facebook, NCT, PANDAS (Pre and Post-Natal Depression Advice and Support) etc will bring you together with like-minded fellow dads and families, and crucially get to the bottom of what's up and discover the root causes. Counselling, other types of talking therapy, and medication can also be a huge help if needed – your GP can discuss these options with you.

Things you can do include:

- Talking to someone you trust – doctor, mates, family member, partner... A problem shared is a problem halved.
- Take some 'me time' – enjoying some time just for you can work wonders, even an hour here and there. A walk, a run, reading a magazine, playing on a console, having a pint with a mate... whatever floats your boat, just get some time out.
- Seek a dad support group – contact your GP surgery, PANDAS, NCT or even social media to find out more.
- Spend some quality time with your baby. Give them a bath, play on the bed together, have a cuddle, read a story – taking time to connect and enjoy your child can really help alleviate any guilt and anxiety.
- Take some exercise each day. Whether it's the gym, a swim, a walk with the buggy – just get outdoors and get those endorphins going, it's a natural mood booster.
- Avoid negative coping strategies such as excessive drinking (so don't overdo it in the pub with your mates), staying away from home, working too much etc, as it will just make things worse.

It's not manly to ignore major stress, depression and anxiety – it's actually more masculine to realise the problem and face it head on. It's easy to be light-hearted and funny about some serious stuff regarding the stress and anxiety of fatherhood, but it's not a game or a joke. Be brave and get a handle on your feelings, otherwise you run the risk of it leading to some real issues with your relationship and parenting. You've got this, you're doing a great job.

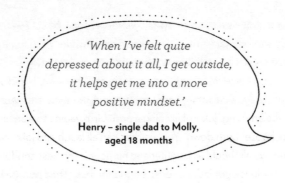

'When I've felt quite depressed about it all, I get outside, it helps get me into a more positive mindset.'

Henry – single dad to Molly, aged 18 months

Let's talk about sex... baby

Finally for this chapter, we delve into the activity that is responsible for all our parenting anxiety in the first place... Sex.

Ahh remember the days before children? Cheeky date nights, stumbling through the front door slightly squiffy, clumsily taking each other's clothes off as you fell into bed for a bit of nookie... Fast forward to post-baby, sitting at opposite ends of the sofa, awkwardly looking at each other, waiting for the other to make the first move.

There is no denying it, the first time you have sex after having a baby is a tense affair for all involved. Women might understandably be anxious about letting anything other than a witch hazel-soaked soothing sanitary pad anywhere near her nethers, but for the guy, it's also an incredibly nerve-wracking time. Questions such as 'will it hurt her?', 'will her bits look and feel the same?', 'what if I can't get it up?' are all real concerns shared with me by real fathers.

My husband I know was really worried about doing it after we'd had Enzo. In his eyes, I had sustained some rather barbaric warfare down there and we've all probably heard the amusing 'joke' of likening a post-birth vagina to watching a bloke's 'favourite boozer burn down'. Yes, we Brits can all laugh and joke, and in fact to a certain extent we all should as laughter and humour is the best antidote to anxiety and awkwardness, but let's not beat around the bush (bad pun, ha ha): the first time you have sex after having a baby is shit – for both of you.

However, sex is important in a healthy relationship, so as anxiety-inducing as it might be for you both, it's key that you talk to each other, find out how the other is feeling about such a prospect (physically and emotionally), and when might be a good time to give it a go. My husband was rather put off by what I might look like – after all, episiotomy stiches aren't the biggest turn-on, I admit. I wasn't exactly swinging from the chandeliers at the prospect either, however, as is often the case, the anticipation was worse than the actual event. I'm not going to lie – it wasn't the most pleasurable of experiences. It was slightly painful, and all I could think of was 'a few months ago I had a baby come out of this!' ... but once we'd 'got it out the way' so to speak, we definitely felt more at ease with each other, and it signalled the start of getting back to some sort of normality – which is always nice.

And remember, it's not all about sex. Start by some good old-fashioned courting and physical contact – a good cuddle is just the *best*, often better actually – and *keep talking to each other*. I wasn't offended by my husband's initial genuine worry about how 'doing it' again might play out, he was being honest, and was scared about how to go about it after me having had an episiotomy – he didn't know how delicate I might be 'down there'. It can be a big deal for a lot of couples and something that has to be dealt with VERY sensitively by talking, sharing and taking the time to explore each other again.

Focusing on what you DO find attractive is important. I also worried about not being as fanciable anymore... my baby tummy and slack pelvic floor weren't exactly the stuff of dreams, however my larger post-pregnancy boobs were a definite thumbs up (once the initial milky leaky mess had settled down). Fortunately, over time, both our fears were, and have been, unfounded, and the result has been an open and humorous approach to our (fairly healthy) physical relationship, which I'm reassured by him hasn't changed in the slightest – in fact being the mother of his child somehow makes me more attractive to him.

Let's get it on

Right, time to remind yourselves that you're not just mummy and daddy. Give these ideas a go in order to ensure you give each other time and attention, and most importantly, enjoy each other!

- Date night! It doesn't matter where you go or what you do – you could even watch a movie at home together – just schedule time together for JUST you two.
- Dress up. Get out of your trackies and baggy own-brand pants – getting spruced up will make you feel so much better, more positive and most definitely more attractive and desirable – this goes for both of you!
- Book a babysitter. Ask parents, relatives, friends to come and sit for a few hours while you get out of the house and enjoy a meal, walk, cinema etc.
- Ban all talk of babies and any other children. Reconnect with the pre-baby you and choose topics that are of mutual interest – holiday ideas, future plans, topical news... anything bar the children! You need a mental rest too.
- Restrict phone usage. Wherever your couple time is spent, try to keep your phones away. Sure, you might need to keep one eye on it in case the babysitter rings, but don't be too beholden to it and allow yourselves time to focus on just each other. The same applies at home – once the evening comes, turn your phone off and instead of scrolling social media, spend time talking to each other.
- Take a walk. Fresh air and a stroll is cheap, easy and can be done any time, anywhere... even if you have to take the baby it can be good-quality couple time and restore feelings of connectivity and togetherness.
- Have a cuddle. Physical contact in any way is really healthy. Instead of feeling like you have to jump into the sack straight away, take any pressure and anxiety off and enjoy some skin-to-skin cuddling and kissing, or even some cheeky foreplay if you have the energy.
- Talk through any fears or anxieties that you might be harbouring within your personal relationship. Keep it positive and exploratory, rather than negative and naggy – once any stresses have been released through sharing, you'll find the physical stuff will become much easier and more enjoyable.

Dr Reetta says...

The challenges of fatherhood

There has been a huge increase in research and interest in fatherhood in the last decade or so. This has followed a shift in Western culture as men have gone from working away from the home and being more detached from family life to being much more involved – while often still working. As a consequence, men can face similar challenges to women in terms of balancing family life and work. It's not as clear cut as just thinking along gender lines when looking into the experiences of fathers vs mothers – it's also very much about their individual differences and experiences. These days, fathers are expected to be involved and hands-on, but may feel unprepared, just as mothers do, too. This can be tough if your father wasn't involved so you don't have him as a modern parenting role model, or if you don't have any male role models in your wider social circles.

In this chapter, Anna has covered post-natal mental health issues in fathers – who can also experience post-natal distress and parenting anxiety. As Anna says, with the changes in responsibilities and expectations, sleep deprivation, changing family dynamics, perhaps lack of control over some aspects of the 'journey', some level of distress is to be expected as you adjust into fatherhood. Fatherhood changes you! Perhaps you have noticed shifts in your values and priorities, and you may have noticed this happening to your partner's priorities too, which may cause tensions. Most parents will struggle adapting to some of the challenges that parenthood presents you with – and that is OK.

In my clinic, conversations about balancing family life and work are central in my work with the men who come to access psychological support. Although when they get in touch the family-work struggle isn't always how the 'presenting problem' is framed, we often discover that it is the key theme, rather than just, let's say, 'work stress'.

It sounds like Anna's husband has adapted to fatherhood well and is very much involved with caring for their baby. As a couple they have communicated about the challenges that have come up, been open about their feelings, and supported each other practically and emotionally. Of course it's not been perfect (it never is!), and we have read about their challenges and disagreements, but they have got through the first year, which is often the toughest time for many new parents. I am guessing Enzo would have developed a healthy bond with both parents, which is one of the most important tasks in the first year and will help him in life as he develops and navigates relationships. He is also learning that a father can be involved with all aspects of a child's life – something that will stay with him if he one day becomes a father himself.

Top tips for new fathers

1. The take-home message is: you are important. Being involved and present is key to your baby's well-being. Nurturing-style fathering (spending quality time with your child and focusing on building a loving, caring relationship) is known to positively influence how well children do in various aspects of their life. Naturally this will come with its challenges, especially if you're balancing work and family needs, including the pressure to provide for your family financially and emotionally. If time is limited, is there one enjoyable activity each week that can become 'your thing' with your baby?

2. Work-life balance for working fathers is equally important as it is for working mothers, but often this is not acknowledged in workplaces, leaving some men feeling their responsibilities as fathers are invisible. Is your fatherhood visible at your workplace? Have you found out about the work-family policies there?

3. The impact of having a baby can affect men in a similar way to how it affects women. Based on this, a lot of the Top Tips in this book are relevant to both mothers and fathers. On the other hand, a father's experience can be different to that of the mother. Men are also known to not seek help as readily as women. If you are feeling depressed, anxious or stressed, consider talking to your GP. In addition, sharing your experiences with your partner, if you have one, or a friend who listens, can be helpful. Do also talk to other fathers about your experiences – it is very likely they will have gone through something similar.

'I couldn't think how I could be relaxed enough for it not to be painful – and indeed it did take a good few months to be able to relax. We have made sure over the last few months to have some date nights. It cannot be underestimated how much this couple time is needed.'

Chloe and Daniel – parents to Willow, aged 12 months

9
THE ROAD AHEAD

The 'what's next' feeling

*The future depends on what
we do in the present.*

Mahatma Gandhi

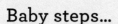

Baby steps...

HELP OTHERS help you. People aren't mind readers so the best thing you can do in keeping as well as possible is to share with people you trust, and tell them how they can help support you best.

KNOW WHAT works for you. It's totally OK to not be perfect – nobody is. If you don't want to do certain things, or you feel safer sticking to what you know, as long as you feel comfortable and in control that's all that matters. Knowing your limits and boundaries is empowering, not a failure.

TAKE EACH DAY as it comes and remind yourself that it's OK to have off days, even totally crap ones – they help us appreciate the good ones even more.

PLAN AHEAD positively. If you're thinking of doing it again and adding to your brood, make sure you let go of any negative feelings from the past and plan ahead in a well-researched, fully supported way.

Peeking through the fog

I think we've established throughout this book that there is one overarching theme, and let's not beat around the bush: being a parent is bloody hard work. Utterly exhausting, repetitive and mind-numbingly boring at times, of course it has its beautiful moments but I'd be lying to you if I didn't tell you there have been times, and frequently still are, when I've felt such overwhelming anger at my new life, my child, my husband, and despair at not knowing what the hell to do about it, that I've genuinely found myself with my head in the sofa cushion having an exasperated scream.

I know I'm not alone in this. One friend I spoke to said she would often walk the local streets with her pushchair, sleep deprived with her sunglasses on, not because it was sunny, but because they shielded the tears rolling down her cheeks. Another mum said she often sought solace in the shower as the noise of the water would drown out her baby's incessant crying – which, as we know, drives all of us more than a little bit crazy at times.

From writing this book, speaking to new mums and dads, and going through it myself, I've realised that pretty much ALL of us feel this way at some time or another. I don't know *anyone* who has escaped unscathed from the trials and tribulations of parenting. Even the competitive mums, when really pressed, admit to sobbing into their coffee, and that actually for all of their social media-ing with glossy filters and perfect-looking days out, being a mum is *not* a walk in the park, and I totally respect their honesty – their 'perfect parent' portrayal is more often than not a coping mechanism. I completely get that... after all, if we 'say' we're having the time of our life, maybe we'll start believing it. I know *I've* been guilty of the 'ooh look at me' posts when underlying them is a fog of post-natal depression that I've simply being trying to fight back at.

All parents reach their wits' end, there's no denying it. And similarly, every parent busks their way through it trying to find their own way.

'My children are chaotic and hilarious. Like me they are dramatic and emotional and I wouldn't have it any other way. Fair to say I underestimated how much joy and love kids can bring you but also how easily they can bring you to your knees!'

Helen Skelton – mum of two boys and TV presenter

I've found that the key to dealing with and getting through each week is to have things to look forward to, little pockets of light to break up each day that will lighten your mood. It can be something as simple as planning a coffee date with a friend once a week, reading a new magazine during nap time, heck, even going out to *buy* the magazine can be a trip and accomplishment in itself, or catching up with your favourite TV programme. Exercise is also hugely important and beneficial to your mental *and* physical well-being. Walks are great, and if you can muster the energy to join a buggy fit or yoga class, then you really will feel the benefits of the feel-good endorphins lifting your mood. Try to book it into your weekly plan as something nice to focus on.

One friend speaks with sheer unbridled excitement about her weekly 'reward' when her mum comes over on a Sunday morning to watch the kids while she enjoys a hot bubble bath and uninterrupted two-hour nap. It is this simple, yet highly coveted prize that gets her through the week. No matter what mummy-hood throws at her, she knows that every seven days she'll get some time to herself and she values it greatly. It doesn't *need* to be a massive activity or outing, it can be anything, just something to break up the monotony, a chance to be 'you', and help to get you through the week: check out the 'Breaking up the Boredom' activity in chapter 6 to give you some ideas.

Activity alert

Let's get physical

Exercise is highly effective in helping to boost our mental health, reducing anxiety and improving our mood. It's also proven to reduce any post-natal depression symptoms. You might not feel like getting out and about and working up a sweat yet, but perhaps have a think about something you might muster up the energy to do – if it's helpful to your mental health, it's gotta be worth a try hasn't it? Always check with your GP that you are fit and well to take up exercise after your birth – it's usually recommended to resume only after the six-week check-up, but do make sure you've been given the all-clear medically.

Here are a few ideas to get you going:

Join a class to which you can take your baby along – mum and baby exercise classes such as buggy fit, baby yoga and Pilates, swimming, aquafitness, mum and baby bootcamp, baby dance etc are all sociable, baby friendly and tailored to suit the capabilities of a mum who has recently given birth.

Ask your health visitor to recommend classes that are happening locally. If they don't know, then check out baby drop-in/weigh-in clinic notice boards for advertisements/flyers of classes, and your local Children's Centre will have suggestions. You can also ask fellow parents for recommendations.

A brisk walk outside pushing the buggy is also extremely good exercise and gets you out of the house, too. It's also a lovely time to engage, smile, and natter away to your little one which helps with baby bonding.

If you can make use of a crèche or babysitter, once you have been given the medical all-clear, have a think about taking part in a gentle aerobic-based exercise class or go swimming – all are great for getting the feel-good endorphins going, but don't stress your ligaments too much or push your body too fast, too soon. Do tell the instructor you've had a baby before the class so they are aware, and can tailor any exercises.

If you are breastfeeding, you'll probably need to wear a really sturdy, supportive sports bra and should try to time your workout so it occurs straight after a feed, before your breasts fill up with milk and become painful when they bounce about.

If you prefer something less energetic and sweaty, why not try yoga, Pilates or mindfulness classes, or just go for a leisurely stroll.

If you can't get out, you could try a home workout using a DVD or an online or app-based exercise programme. Ensure you've been given the all-clear by a medical practitioner and start slowly with a gentle and appropriate home workout (there are loads of post-natal workouts online so have a look into what feels right for you). It's really important you don't push yourself too hard to start with and take into account the fact that your joints will be more prone to damage post-birth due to the ligaments still being looser than usual (this happens to enable the pelvis to open up during childbirth and takes a little while to go back to normal).

You've got this – coping YOUR way

Whatever your birth and parenting journey, it's important to find what works for you and not measure yourself against others... believe me, it rarely serves you well and in mine and so many other parents' experiences, only leaves you feeling bad about yourself.

> *'You want to be the best you can be for your baby... and here's the thing, you will be. You are all they know. You learn how to parent together. If you make a mistake, they let you know pretty quickly and you also develop your own mother-baby shorthand, which may be very different to your friends'.'*
>
> **Jenni Falconer – TV presenter and mum to Ella**

A lot of mums have told me they feel inadequate and threatened in certain situations with other parents. Have you ever tried to have a shower and put make-up on for a mum and baby class? Let me tell you, I have, but honestly I rarely succeed – the best you get from me these days is a courtesy spray of deodorant and my hair brushed – personally I don't give a toss what other parents might think (well, probably I do a bit but I'm too busy juggling the baby/bag/pushchair/being on time to properly care). Lots of us do feel pressured at some point to 'look the part', though. To quote one:

'I wish every mum would
just turn up looking like they've been
pulled through a hedge backwards, with puke
on their shoulder and three-day-old mascara
smudged under their eye bags. Just every now and
again. Just so I don't feel like the only frazzled mess.'

Zara – mum of twins Ace and Annabel, aged 15 months

It's not just about appearances: we're all trying to work out what type of parent we are, too. Some of us model ourselves on our own parents' methods and values, and others, depending on their upbringing, do the complete opposite. You may have had a happy childhood during which your parents showered you with love and disciplined you kindly and fairly, you may have had parents who were distracted or disinterested in your childhood, found it hard to be a parent, and who perhaps didn't make the right choices for you... Whatever our childhood journey, it impacts the way *we* parent. We compare and contrast our own experiences and it serves to influence and mould what's important to us in parenting our own kids.

A mum told me how her mother was highly critical towards her from an early age and even though she knows she was loved, it just served to knock her confidence. Now, as a parent, she ensures she praises and encourages her children frequently to avoid creating the same issues she developed. Another dad speaks fondly of how his parents were sticklers for minding your Ps and Qs and were big fans of eating around the dinner table all together – something he now ensures he also does with his own kids as he recognises how beneficial it was for him as a kid growing up.

233

'At times I get extremely worried and nervous for them as this is a crazy world we live in. They completely depend on me and my husband so I put pressure on myself to be the best mum I can possibly be... But worrying too much gets you nowhere.'

Una Healy – popstar and mum of two

Essentially we take the good and not-so-good bits from our own childhood, nick a few ideas from other role models we have in our lives (such as grandparents or friend's parents) to form our own way of being what we hope is a good parent. Asking your own folks about how it was for them all those years ago can also be hugely helpful and a bit of an eye-opener in understanding that parenting is something we ALL go into blindly. Becoming a grown-up is weird isn't it? I'm not sure when it happens, but there comes a point when you stop being a kid and realise that your parents are actually just normal mistake-making human beings (and not Superpeople). Growing up it may have seemed as though your mum or dad knew *exactly* what they were doing, had the whole 'being a parent' thing nailed, but why not have a chat with them? Chances are they'll admit to busking the whole parenting malarkey just like you – and that was without the helpful crutch of Google, social media and WhatsApp to help us overcome our fears and fumbles – heck it was even before mobile phones!

Being a parent is completely unique to you. Save yourself a whole heap of unnecessary anxiety and low self-esteem by having the confidence to accept that you're doing parenting 'your' way. And that means working out what you need in order to cope – hopefully in a happy and positive way.

FRONT   BACK

> 'Being a parent is challenging.
> I struggle to find the right answers
> or how to solve a problem without a raised
> voice or a threat I don't follow through. But the
> thing is, we can't beat ourselves up about it. You've
> just gotta pat yourself on the back and be thankful
> that you haven't throttled your husband yet, ha ha.'
>
> **Michelle Heaton – TV personality,**
> **popstar and mum of two**

The big question...

If you haven't yet, it's a question you're going to be asked sooner or later... and one that might be tricky to answer, particularly if you've had a less-than-ideal first birth experience. That question is of course, 'Would you have another one?' A lot of first-time mums I interviewed for this book were left with negative feelings towards their first births – yes, a few had lovely experiences, but the majority were left feeling a bit blank about the whole experience and often couldn't remember parts of it. The prospect of having another baby can be all too terrifying to contemplate, particularly if you've been left with any negative feelings that need resolving before you even think about doing it again. The same is of course true for parents of more than one child who are thinking about having a third, fourth, fifth, sixth...

Birth reflections

Birth reflections can be so important for a good recovery from birth trauma. This NHS service may be called something slightly different in different areas, such as birth afterthoughts, debriefs or birth stories, but you should be able to arrange one wherever you live in the UK either through your health visitor, GP or by directly contacting the Supervisor of Midwives at the place where you gave birth. You can also contact The Birth Trauma Association, who can help with finding the right location and professional for you. They also offer a closed Facebook group, which can be hugely helpful in being able to share your story on a safe monitored platform, surrounded by like-minded mums who can listen and empathise: www. facebook.com/groups/TheBTA.

Birth reflections are a chance to talk over and debrief your birth experience with a midwife who has been specifically trained for the job. This is something I hugely benefitted from after my less-than-perfect birth, as six months on I still couldn't let go of some of the negativity I felt towards it, and I'd 'lost' patches of time during my stay in hospital in the immediate aftermath. Other mums have told me how helpful it was to put to rest any bad feelings or get answers to questions they had, and the majority say it made them more proud of their birth story and meant they more fully understood the decisions made at the time. It is recommended that you book a birth reflection within the first year after giving birth, purely for ease of locating hospital notes, but it's not essential as they will always be kept in an archive.

> *'My health visitor suggested I might benefit from a birth reflection to help ease the feelings of anxiety and disappointment I held about my labour. I want another baby but felt scared about doing it again in case things went wrong. The session was really helpful. I now feel much more positive about doing it a second time.'*
>
> **Brooke – mum of Gemma, aged 11 months**

How to... book a birth reflection

CONTACT YOUR local health visitor service, GP or the hospital you gave birth at, and ask to be put in touch with the maternity department. Once through, ask to speak to whoever deals with birth reflections, sometimes called birth debriefs or afterthoughts.

YOU WILL BE offered an appointment and this will be given by a specially trained midwife, specifically tasked with taking women through their births and answering any questions they might have in order to help you process what happened.

THE APPOINTMENT takes place in a private office, usually in the maternity department, and is a little like a counselling session in that you will often be given an hour to talk through everything. Partners are welcome to attend, too. You might feel you'd like some support, or they might also benefit from the debrief.

THE HOSPITAL will have sourced all your medical birth notes from the time of your labour, and the midwife will take you through each part of your experience, bit by bit, allowing you to process it in your own time.

YOU ARE INVITED to ask any questions and offload any emotions – the aim is for you to leave feeling listened to and with a better understanding of your labour, and hopefully feeling more positive about the experience. You are welcome to leave feedback, too.

Next time around

This might be WAY too soon for you depending on what stage of the baby journey you're at, but at some point you might tussle with the idea of doing it all again. If another child is on your wish list, you might feel differently about how you would do it a second or third time around, certainly if you've already experienced a less-than-perfect birth.

Overall, vaginal births are generally considered by health professionals to be the safer option for mum and baby, but an increasing amount of women are opting for elective, sometimes called planned, Caesarians. The most recent figures from the National Childbirth Trust show that there has been a rise in the number of elective Caesarians to around one in eight of all births. These planned procedures are perhaps more commonly associated with women and babies who are physically at risk going through a vaginal birth, such as baby being in tricky position (eg breech), if you suffer from conditions such as placenta praevia (placenta blocking the opening of the cervix), or if you're having multiple babies.

It's a topic that is in the midst of some controversy, since many medical experts recommend a vaginal birth, if possible, because it is considered to be of lower risk *physically* to mum and baby. However, according to NICE guidelines you have the right to choose a C-section if that is your preference, and an increasing number of women who suffer with extreme anxiety, birth phobias (see chapter 2), or who have had a traumatic birth are opting to give birth this way the next time.

C-section OR V-birth

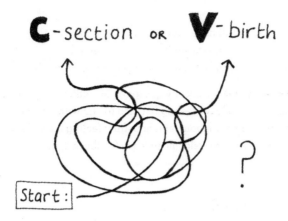

Start:

Speak to your GP and midwife so they can refer you to a consultant to discuss your reasons and options available. If for any reason your consultant refuses you should ask to be referred to another consultant for the procedure. You will probably find that your midwife and/or consultant will want to talk through your birth choice with you, to make sure that you fully understand the risks and benefits associated with vaginal birth and C-section. This isn't necessarily to 'talk you into' having your baby one way or the other, but to ensure you are making a fully informed choice about the best way for you to give birth. They may well recommend one way – and let's be frank, C-sections carry a significant cost factor to the NHS, not to mention the recovery time involved (it is, after all, a major operation) – but ultimately how you have your baby is your choice.

A lot of mums I spoke to who had gone through a planned Caesarian spoke positively about the experience, and found their requests were heard and respected.

Here is Alex's story:

'I had a terrible birth with my first baby. It was a long and slow labour and the birth ended in forceps delivery. My baby was healthy but the trauma of the birth stayed with me for a long time afterwards, I developed panic attacks and was terrified about having another baby. I got pregnant again two years later, I was happy about the pregnancy but all my fears reached fever pitch about having to go through giving birth again, I was highly anxious. After speaking to my midwife and doctor, I decided I wanted to be in control of my birth as much as I could. It was the lack of control and the unknown that made my anxiety worse. I was referred to an NHS consultant and it was agreed that I could have a planned C-section at 39 weeks. Knowing that I had a 'date' really helped me relax and enjoy the rest of my pregnancy. The night before I had my second son, I had dinner with my husband and went to bed early. It was weird to think I was having a baby the next day. At 6am the next morning I was driven to hospital, we were shown to our room, and after a few hours I was told 'it was time' and I actually walked to the theatre... it was all so calm. I had a drip put in my arm and then was given the spinal block anaesthetic (which didn't hurt as I had a local one put in first), then it was all systems go, screen went up, a lot of tugging and suction noises, and eight minutes later my baby boy was out! It was the most calm and relaxed atmosphere, I felt reassured and in control of all that was going on, and quite frankly, compared to the first birth, it was a picnic! Having an elective C-section was the best decision I made – for me, the baby and my mental health.'

Alex – mum of two

The NICE guidelines state that, after exploring the mother's reasons, and offering alternative suggestions, if it is her wish, an elective, or planned, Caesarian should be offered. However, it's worth noting that NICE guidelines, while important, are only guidance and hospitals do not need to follow them. There is also no legal obligation for a doctor to perform a procedure that they do not think is in the patient's best interest.

If you would like to explore the option of an elective Caesarian, do speak to your GP, midwife or health professional, be prepared to weigh up all the options, but ultimately be firm about your wishes.

Doing it differently

Whether you choose to give birth naturally (vaginally), or have a Caesarian, there are things you can do to help support yourself even more before, during and after birth that you might like to look into and consider.

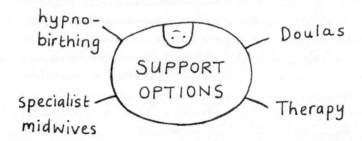

Doulas

A doula is a woman who gives support, help, and advice to another woman during pregnancy, and during and after the birth.

A doula can help a pregnant woman during her pregnancy, and all through labour and birth, and can be a support in the post-natal phase too. They are a trained and experienced birth/parenting-support professional, and can often recognise some of the signs if something needs addressing, such as more than 'just' the baby blues, mastitis (infection in the breast), infected stitches, that kind of thing, and can ensure the mother gets any extra help she needs as soon as possible.

Doulas do not take a clinical role and work alongside midwives and doctors. They do not advise, but can support a woman to find balanced information to make informed decisions about her maternity care.

Birth doulas go 'on call' 24/7 towards the end of your pregnancy, and will support you during labour and birth whenever you need them. Post-natal doulas provide flexible practical and emotional support for mothers and families in their own homes. Some specialise, while others work as both birth and post-natal doulas.

It can be a little on the pricey side to employ a doula (it's a private service). Costs for a birth doula vary greatly depending on the area they work in, how experienced they are, how much time they spend with you, and what they include in the fee, but you can expect to pay £600–£2000. A post-natal doula is around £15–£30 per hour, but if you would benefit from the help, support and comfort that a doula can offer, it can be more than worth it to save up the pennies. www.doula.org.uk has loads of information if you'd like to find out more.

Hypnobirthing

Hypnobirthing is a complete birth-education programme that teaches simple but specific self-hypnosis, relaxation and breathing techniques for a better birth.

Hypnobirthing is much more than just self-hypnosis or hypnotherapy for childbirth. It's a technique that helps you to discover that severe pain does not have to be an accompaniment to labour. You'll learn how to release the fears and anxieties you may have about giving birth and how to overcome previous traumatic births, and you will also be taught how to put yourself back in control of your birth – rather than blindly turning your birthing experience over to your doctor or midwife.

Hypnobirthing doesn't mean you'll be in a trance or asleep. It's about relaxation and you'll be able to chat, and be in good spirits, totally relaxed, but fully in control. And you'll always be aware of what is happening to you. There are plenty of books, podcasts and websites that contain helpful information, so if it's something you might like to explore you can check these out and/or take a look at www. thewisehippo.com or www.hypnobirthing.co.uk.

It's important to note that 'on the day' your birth situation may dictate how effective (or not) you are at being able to put hypnobirthing into practice. I managed to effectively utilise my hypnobirthing breathing and visualisation techniques and soothing MP3s during the final weeks of pregnancy to keep calm and prepare, and also in the first part of my labour at home, but due to Enzo's complicated position and subsequent birth interventions, in the end I lost the will to live, let alone the focus to 'breathe my baby out'. I did however always retain and put into practice the empowerment part you're taught, ensuring we asked questions along the way and attempted to stay in control of the birth as much as we were able in the early phases.

'I recommend hypnobirthing to everyone. The relaxing MP3s became a firm favourite of my partner's and mine before I even gave birth, and on the day the relaxation and visualisation techniques really helped in coping with the pain and doing it my way. It was a really positive experience for me and helped me focus on the job in hand'

Chloe – mum to Serena, aged 7 months

Private and specialist midwives

If money is no object, you could look into getting your own private midwife to accompany and support you from the moment you conceive right through to the post-natal care for you and baby. A private midwife is able to build a close and trusting relationship with you and provide continuity of care. Having the same experienced and skilled person to care for you throughout has been widely reported to have better outcomes for you and baby, with a big study carried out by the global health research network, Cochrane Collaboration, citing that women who know their midwives before birth, ie during pregnancy, are less likely to have an assisted birth. The NCT reports that two thirds of women who had gotten to know their midwife before birthing, said that as a result they felt more relaxed, confident and safer.

A private midwife helps to put together an 'ideal scenario' birth plan that works for you (but can help to manage expectations too as we know that babies are unpredictable little pickles), and she will ensure everything is explained to you and your wishes are respected. She will also work alongside you to adapt to choices you would like to make – whether it is a home birth, or private or NHS hospital.

The cost of a private midwife varies from £150 for a single ante- or post-natal appointment, to £2000 for a birth support package, to £500 for a week of post-natal home care. www.privatemidwives.com is a good website to get an idea of what this route can offer.

You can also tap into your local NHS midwifery services. Ask your GP or midwife if you have maternal mental health midwives in your area. The Royal College of Midwives agrees that all maternity units need to have a specialist maternal mental health midwife on staff, so although one *might* not be available or guaranteed, it's well worth asking as more and more are being recruited by the NHS to help women in need of specialist care during pregnancy, birth and afterwards.

If you're mega loaded, and don't mind someone else feeding (by bottle I mean) or settling your baby during the witching hours, then Maternity Nurses are an option. A Maternity Nurse is a trained and experienced nurse or nanny who specialises in the care of newborns. The aim is to help a mother and baby settle and get into a routine with sleep and feeding in the early weeks and months. Costing around £180-£220 for a single baby per 24 hours (for multiples it's more), it's not cheap, and of course you will need to provide a bed for your nurse so she can rest. If you're not a fan of routine it might not be for you though as they do tend to practise pretty strict routines.

In addition to 24 hour maternity nurses, there are also sleep nannies/trainers (to help get your baby/toddler into a good sleep pattern), and night nannies (you hire them to literally come for the night time shift to enable you a full night's sleep – Holy Grail!). Prices for both really do vary depending on the agency, location, how many babies you have and how long you need them for – roughly it starts around £115 and can go up to anything around the £200 per day/night mark. You will probably reach a stage at some point when you really can't put a price on a precious night's sleep, but do your research and crunch the numbers to ensure you don't put any financial strain on yourself if you decide to explore any of these options.

Therapy

Talking therapy is hugely effective in that it offers support, and a confidential space in which to talk through your feelings, thoughts and worries in pregnancy. A lot of therapists are trained in pregnancy-related mental health so check out www.bacp. co.uk or www.NHS.co.uk to find a suitable professional, or ask your GP for a referral to an appropriate counsellor or therapist.

How to... get in the zone

Giving birth is a process that is full of uncertainties, and that can make us feel nervous, excited, worried, scared, anxious... a whole cocktail of emotions. Often it's the lack of control over the situation that can ramp up our anxiety even more. Try these handy pointers, or pass them on to an expecting friend, to help prepare for the job in hand in hopefully a relaxing way:

INSTEAD OF thinking about the what ifs, focus your mind on what you CAN control: your preferred choices on birth (ie on a bed, in water), birthing positions, pain-relief options, and be sure that everyone knows your wishes. Your preferences are yours, but as birth is the unknown and often takes a bit of an unexpected turn, have a think about what it might be like IF things don't go the way you ideally hope, and how you might feel about that.

CLOSE YOUR eyes and focus on your baby in your tummy, and remind yourself of the care and support you have around you and your baby, in order to ensure you both emerge healthy and well. Whatever path you end up taking, be safe in the knowledge that people are here to help you.

TAKE A nice deep breath, imagine that there is a large velvety protective cloak around you, and in any moment of 'eek', while you have this cloak on, nothing is going to unsettle or upset you. Block out any unhelpful noise or opinions and, nice and calmly, keep focusing on the end goal – your baby.

KEEP AN open mind. Be empowered to ask all the questions you want. Ultimately this is your birth experience – embrace it.

Message from a Midwife

Whatever you might decide to do the next time around (*if* there is a next time) it's also important to remember that NHS midwives and health professionals really are, in the main, amazing, and worth their weight in gold, doing their jobs in often tricky circumstances. Having spoken to many midwives while writing this book, I think this lovely one sums up how it really isn't ever 'them and us', in fact we're all one united birthing team doing the best we can:

'I have been privileged to meet lots of amazing families and beautiful babies. There's nothing more rewarding for a midwife than seeing the look of pride, amazement and joy on a new mum's face as she realises that she has just brought a new life into the world and as she first sets eyes on her beautiful baby, or the moment when a family you have supported throughout their pregnancy introduce you to their newest addition. While the pressures and strains under which the NHS operates are very real, these moments are the ones which inspire us to continue to do what we do.

I've attended hundreds of births; homebirths, 'normal' births, ones where forceps or ventouse have been used and caesarean sections, which have all been special in their own way. My aim is always to enable a woman and her family to feel empowered by their birth experience.

"Healthy mum, healthy baby" is a phrase which is often quoted. While it's true that making sure both are physically safe is key, it is also important to consider the impact birth can have on a family's emotional health. While I've been involved in lots of births where it has been a positive and empowering experience for the mum and her family, sadly this isn't always the case. Emergencies can occur unexpectedly, or maybe things don't quite happen as you had thought. The fear and disempowerment this can sometimes lead to is very real and it's important to recognise this. If you've had a

difficult experience, it's easy to try and sweep it under the carpet, particularly with all the demands that having a new baby brings, but it's important not to hide it.

Hospitals often offer a 'Birth reflection' service, where you can chat to a midwife or a doctor about your experience, discussing what happened and why certain decisions were made. This can be particularly helpful if you are planning on having another child, as they often offer appointments when you are pregnant to put plans in place, to try to help you feel more supported throughout your next pregnancy and birth.

No matter what your experience though, it is important to be kind to yourself. Emotional and mental health is just as important as physical health.'

Joanna Brown – Midwife at Guys and St Thomas' Hospital London

The road ahead

I think we're all agreed that nothing really can prepare you for the monumental life change of becoming a mum or dad. It doesn't matter how many books you read, programmes you watch or podcasts you listen to, going from zero to one (or more) has to be the biggest life wallop ever, as your world is turned upside down and inside out in one fell swoop. Going from your first child to more is still pretty pant-wettingly scary but at least you know a little bit of a) what to expect and b) what to do to keep a small human alive, and you can hopefully take some comfort in the fact that you'll never have to make that transition from non-parent to parent ever again. Whatever your offspring throw at you (literally, when you get to the terrible twos) you never have to endure that mind-boggling phase of redefining yourself as A PARENT. Whether you have one, or eight... it's all pretty terrifying, overwhelming and downright weird at times, but I hope at some point you're also able to enjoy, appreciate and love the incredible human beings that you brilliantly, and unselfishly, care for, and the amazing parent you are – you wouldn't have picked this book up if you didn't care.

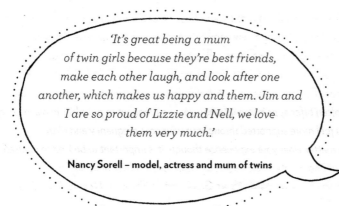

'It's great being a mum of twin girls because they're best friends, make each other laugh, and look after one another, which makes us happy and them. Jim and I are so proud of Lizzie and Nell, we love them very much.'

Nancy Sorell – model, actress and mum of twins

On the day my baby was born my life changed forever. At 6.55pm on a sunny but chilly September evening, I became a mum. At the time it was impossible to fathom, and in those early weeks in particular I bloody hated and resented it at times. I know that loads of other parents feel like this and the worry and guilt many of us carry around is just so unnecessary, because we're real.

Even though there are often times when we feel knackered, lack even the most basic of parenting skills, are riddled with sleep-deprived anxiety and feel totally incompetent, we need to make sure we stop frequently, go easy on ourselves and appreciate the good, countless wonderful, moments – for there are many, even if we have to search a little bit. And as the months and years go on, there *will* be plenty more. We should be proud of the parent we are, and enjoy the little legacy we have created.

We are all troopers, we are all amazing, and we all have one incredible thing in common... we are all parents. And what a brilliantly bespoke crazy club it is.

Dr Reetta says...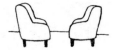

Keeping an open mind Although having a baby is commonplace, it's also complicated. As part of becoming a parent you are very likely to experience some parenting anxiety as you go through the years ahead. How high the levels of anxiety are, how it impacts on your day-to-day life and how long it lasts for will depend on who you are, including your circumstances, coping strategies and support network. I hope through reading this book you can take away the key message: parenting anxiety is normal, expected and something that we *all* experience. Anxiety is everywhere, so the task isn't to get rid of it but, like Anna has done, learn to cope with it.

Use the tools and tips in this book to help you approach parenthood with an open, accepting mind, rather than thinking there are definite, one-size-fits-all answers or guidance. As is often said, being a parent is a job that's never finished. One way to think about your new role is that you are as old as your baby is – the birth of a first baby equals the birth of a parent. As your baby develops, so will you, and the process can't be hurried. As part of this process, we should all accept that being a parent is rewarding *and* exhausting; exciting *and* boring; and enjoyable *and* difficult.

Depending on where you are in your parenting journey, you may or may not have got to know yourself as a parent, including what your strengths, weaknesses and triggers for anxiety are. You may be surprised by what you thought you would find easy or hard and that has ended up being the opposite. You may find the baby months very tough, but enjoy the toddler years, or vice versa. You may be positively surprised by how well one aspect of parenting is going, but disappointed or upset about another aspect that isn't going well at all.

Top tips for the road ahead

1. Being mindful of your own emotions is an essential part of parenting. Observe yourself, not judgementally, but with an open mind. Notice what you are feeling during the tough moments and days. Practise pausing before responding: stop what you are doing, breathe or take a few minutes to yourself, and then re-gather your thoughts. How would you like to learn to respond to the situation you are in?

2. As Anna says, no amount of reading, watching or talking prepares you for parenthood. Indeed, recent research by Swansea University links reading too many prescriptive baby books (that give advice on strict routines) to increased feelings of depression. Many new parents, however, want to read books, as it can be comforting to have that 'guidance'. Keep enjoying reading, if it's your thing, but be aware of reading too much (it's quite possible to sign up to too many parenting emails/blogs etc) and becoming overwhelmed by often-opposing advice. My personal favourite parenting book is Naomi Stadlen's *What Mothers Do: Especially when it looks like nothing*. Or if you want something a bit more 'how-to', Sarah Ockwell-Smith is an author who gives practical, gentle guidance on various aspects of parenting.

3. As Anna and I have expressed throughout the book: *there isn't one right way to parent*. You need to learn what works for *you*. Trust yourself and your instincts, and do what you think is the best. Then, find people (face to face or on online) around you who are supportive and think about parenting with them. Finally, as Anna says, dedicate some time to just 'be' with your baby – enjoy getting to know them and their unique personality.

Sometimes parents need a little bit of help, whether it is thinking about their well-being or something about parenting, or to have a space in which to reflect on their thoughts and feelings. There are a number of organisations and professionals that can help with this – see the Resources section at the end of the book.

RESOURCES

For mental health help and support

Anxiety UK – www.anxietyuk.org.uk Infoline: 08444 775 774

Samaritans – www.samaritans.org Freephone: 116 123 Email: jo@samaritans.org

SANE – www.sane.org.uk Saneline: 0300 304 7000

Mind – www.mind.org.uk Helpline: 0300 123 3393

Birth Trauma Association – www.birthtraumaassociation.org.uk General enquiries: 01264 860 380

APP Network (Action on Postpartum Psychosis) – www.app-network.org General enquiries: 020 3322 9900 Email: app@app-network.org

Postpartum Support International – www.postpartum.net Email: support@postpartum.net

NHS – www.NHS.uk NHS 111 number available 24/7: 111

Maternal Mental Health Network – www.maternalmentalhealthnetwork.org.uk

Maternal Mental Health Alliance – www.maternalmentalhealthalliance.org

PANDAS Foundation UK (Pre and Post Natal Depression Advice and Support) – www.pandasfoundation.org.uk Tel: 0843 28 98 401

PANDAS dads' Facebook group: www.facebook.com/pandasdads

TAMBA – Twins and Multiple Births Association https://www.tamba.org.uk/document.doc?id=279

Family, parent and birth support

Home-Start – www.home-start.org.uk Tel: 0116 464 5490 Email: info@home-start.org.uk

Doula UK – www.doula.org.uk Tel: 0871 433 3103 Email: info@doula.org.uk

Private Midwives – www.privatemidwives.com Tel: 0800 470 2103 Email: info@privatemidwives.com

NCT (National Childbirth Trust) – www.nct.org.uk Tel: 0300 330 0700 Email: enquiries@nct.org.uk

Antenatal Online – www.antenatalonline.co.uk Email: louise@antenatalonline.co.uk

Sure Start Children's Centres – www.gov.uk/find-sure-start-childrens-centre Tel: 0370 000 2288

Citizens Advice Bureau – www.citizensadvice.org.uk Tel: 03454 04 05 06

Channel Mum – www.channelmum.com

Mumsnet – www.mumsnet.com Email: contactus@mumsnet.com

Netmums – www.netmums.com Email: contactus@netmums.com

Baby Centre – www.babycentre.co.uk

Dad Info – www.dad.info

Fatherhood Institute - www.fatherhoodinstitute.org

ACKNOWLEDGEMENTS

Taking on the task of writing another book so soon after giving birth was always going to be a massive challenge, but I have relished the past six months of being a multi-tasking working mum of one. There has been a lot of tea, packets of biscuits, and more than a couple of sleep deprived 'writer's block' meltdowns when I've been 'that' close to lobbing my laptop out of a moving car window.

However, here we are, I'm delighted to have completed this book and am incredibly proud of all the hard work that has gone into it, with the help of a lot of lovely people.

Mum, Dad and Liz, without your plentiful babysitting and constant support, this book quite simply would not have been written. You're the best grandparents in the world for Little Man. I am indebted to you, thank you.

My wonderful agent, and Super mum, Samantha – thank you for your unrelenting support, help, and belief in me. I am blessed to have an amazing friend and agent in you. Claire, the most loyal publicist in the world – thank you for always going above and beyond.

My editor Charlotte, the most incredible, eagle-eyed, creative, and downright knowledgeable woman I know. Your encouragement, ideas and passion for this topic have been instrumental in the book becoming what it is. Thank you for keeping me on track, and trusting in what I wanted to achieve with this book. Copy editor, Lucy – your input at the latter stages has been the icing on the cake – such valuable advice and I'm honoured you decided to work on my book. Also a huge thank you to *all* the Bloomsbury Team, Sarah, Lizzy, Henry, Katherine... best publishing team ever.

Reetta, I am blessed to know you and am honoured you agreed to do yet another book with me. I couldn't do it without you or your wisdom and expertise, you're an amazing woman and fellow mum.

To my wonderful Mummy and Daddy friends – thank you for being a huge part of this book and trusting me with your innermost thoughts, feelings and experiences. You have all humbled me, I am so fortunate to know you, and I am honoured to be able to share your valuable stories with other mums and dads.

My husband Alex, thanks for being my teammate and helping me in getting this book written. Looking after our son, juggling work, and making sure we all eat... you're the best hubby and daddy in the world – ti amo per sempre bello.

And last, but certainly not least, my precious Vincenzo George, my biggest thank you goes to you my darling son. Without you, this book simply wouldn't have been written. I love you more than I ever thought possible. Your arrival into the world wasn't in the way I'd hoped, it wasn't either of our 'fault', just one of those things and thank goodness you came out safely, I am thankful every day that you did. I had a few hiccups in those early days and weeks, but you are without question, the best thing I have ever done. My most perfect creation and the apple of my eye.

Regardless of how honest and open I am in this book about some pretty rubbish and upsetting feelings, and it's important I *am* because I want to help other mummys and daddys like me, I need you to know that you were, and are, totally worth it. I truly love you with a gut-wrenching emotion words couldn't ever do justice to. You are perfect, and you are mine. I hope in years to come you'll be as proud of your old Mum as I am of you.

INDEX

Index